Awakening To *Love*

Journey *of the* Heart

**CHANNELING THE
TEACHERS OF THE LIGHT**

Darren Marc

Copyright © 2021 by Heart Light Publishing

All rights reserved. No part of this publication may be reproduced, distributed, or transmitted in any form or by any means, including photocopying, recording, or other electronic or mechanical methods, without the prior written permission of the publisher, except in the case of brief quotations embodied in critical reviews and certain other noncommercial uses permitted by copyright law. For permission requests, contact the publisher at the email address: darrenmarc111@gmail.com.

Printed in the United States of America

ISBN: 9780578980058 (Paperback)

ISBN: 9780578980065 (eBook)

Library of Congress Control Number: 2021917827

First Edition

10 9 8 7 6 5 4 3 2 1

Table of Contents

An Introduction from the Teachers of the Light v
About the Channel vii
Who We Are viii

CHAPTER 1	The Human Incarnation	11
CHAPTER 2	Retreating into Your Heart	21
CHAPTER 3	Seeing with New, Improved Eyes	35
CHAPTER 4	Our Prophecy	43
CHAPTER 5	The Celebration	45
CHAPTER 6	Manifestation	51
CHAPTER 7	The Great Remembering	59
CHAPTER 8	Be Unproductive	63
CHAPTER 9	Prayer	71
CHAPTER 10	Your Soul Mission	79
CHAPTER 11	Unleash Your Inner Child	87
CHAPTER 12	Sacred Mornings	91
CHAPTER 13	A Day of Reception	99
CHAPTER 14	Recalibrating the Heart	103
CHAPTER 15	Sitting in Appreciation	107
CHAPTER 16	Love Heals All Wounds	111
CHAPTER 17	Let Go and Flow	119
CHAPTER 18	Receiving Divine Guidance	125
CHAPTER 19	Tuning the Heart	131
CHAPTER 20	Finding the One	137

CHAPTER 21	The End of Separation	139
CHAPTER 22	Slow Down	145
CHAPTER 23	Receive the Gift	147
CHAPTER 24	The Best Kind of Spirituality	155
CHAPTER 25	Blossom Like a Flower	159
CHAPTER 26	Your Purpose for Being Here	163
CHAPTER 27	Stilling the Mind	167
CHAPTER 28	Higher, Higher, Higher	175
CHAPTER 29	Stay High	179
CHAPTER 30	Your Garden of Gifts	187
CHAPTER 31	Vibrational Shifting	193
CHAPTER 32	Embrace the Change	197
CHAPTER 33	Love, Strength, and Power	201
CHAPTER 34	Vibrational Awareness	207
CHAPTER 35	Suffering	209
CHAPTER 36	There Is Greatness Inside You	213
CHAPTER 37	Nonjudgment	215
CHAPTER 38	Keep Going	217
CHAPTER 39	The Human Experience	221
CHAPTER 40	Sacred Moments	225
CHAPTER 41	Laughter Is the Best Medicine	233
CHAPTER 42	Falling in Love	237
CHAPTER 43	Now Is the Time	241
CHAPTER 44	Conscious Creation	249
CHAPTER 45	Be Receptive	253
CHAPTER 46	A Momentous Occasion	259

An Introduction from the Teachers of the Light

Dearest friends,
There is a great love that is present in your heart. This love that we speak of is your god-presence. It is the presence of god that lives inside of you.

Isn't it ironic that many of you go searching everywhere, looking in every corner of the world for this god? And yet, it has always been and will always be inside your own heart. You might say, indeed, the creator is playing a game of hide and go seek with you. But the creator is hiding in the last place many of you choose to look, your own heart.

For many of you on this Earth plane, it's quite an arduous journey to know the depths of love you have in your heart. But once you begin to get a taste of it, you will never want to return to anything else you have experienced in your life. Your life will never be the same, and this love will guide you throughout your life. You will truly become the I AM that I AM presence embodied in a physical form.

This is what every great teacher who has been on this planet has taught. So, we're here to teach it to you again in a different way with different words. But the teaching is no different. It's the same teaching that has been taught since the beginning of time and will continue to be taught until the end of time, although there really is no time. It is the same teaching that will continue to be taught until all have returned to love, until all know themselves as they *truly* are, and until all know the god-spark that exists within themselves and the love that is in their own hearts.

And so dear friends, in this book, we invite you to go on a journey of the heart with us. Allow us and the channel to take you by the hand and guide you to the place you so desperately seek to be in, a place that is inside you.

About the Channel

Many of you might ask how it is that we speak through the channel.

The channel has been on his own path of finding the love that is in *his* heart. And he has raised his vibration to a place where he can now be receptive to the words we speak through him. It is only through love that he has raised his vibration. It is only through knowing the love that is in his heart that he has enabled himself to be a channel for these words that we speak.

And so, it is our wish that all of you who are reading these words will come to feel this vibration and come to know the love in *your* hearts. And please know that all of you who read these words have the ability to be receptive to words, ideas, and guidance that comes from the divine.

Who We Are

Many of you might also ask who it is that we are. We are a group of spirit guides who now exist solely in the higher realms. We have incarnated into physical forms before, but we have no need to do it anymore. We are simply content to be in the space we are in. We have the ability to take on form if and when we need to. But we do not do it in a physical body like yours. We do it in what we call a light body, simply a body made of energy.

The channel allows himself to receive our words and to speak them with his voice. As this occurs, his consciousness is still present. But as he likes to say, it is in the passenger seat, simply observing as the words flow. We use his vocabulary. We choose to speak simply, not in riddles and not in rhymes, but in language you'll easily understand.

And we ask you not only to read the words but to actually have the intention of tuning in to the energetic signature that is part of the words. For there is a particular vibration, a particular energy, that is inherent in these words that will allow you to enter into your own heart with more ease. So, we encourage you, every time you open this book to read, simply state out loud or silently to yourself:

- *I read with the intention of absorbing the energetic frequency of these words in my heart and in my soul.*
- *I allow myself to receive what spirit wants me to hear.*

- *I allow myself to receive what spirit wants me to feel.*
- *I allow myself to receive what spirit wants me to know.*

We begin with chapter one—The Human Incarnation.

CHAPTER 1

The Human Incarnation

Many of you ask, "What am I doing here? How did I get here? This place is crazy!" ☺ You chose to come here, my friends. There's an adventure at hand, and you are part of it. We want to begin by honoring you and celebrating you for the choice you made to be here at this time of awakening. It was a brave choice, and we honor you. Not all are so brave. So, know that simply by having chosen to be here—to have shown up—that you are one of the brave ones.

We do not wish to get into many details about a human incarnation, but just know that you are a soul and that you have chosen as spirit to embody a physical form. There is a play at hand. Perhaps some of you enjoy going to the theater as the channel does. In fact, he quite enjoys participating in the theater, as well. It is one of his great passions. Indeed, there will be a chapter in this book about expression.

> *You are all here to express the god-presence that's inside of you.*

And so, we say *that* is the purpose of a human incarnation. It is to express the god-presence within you—nothing less and nothing more. For indeed, many of you have forgotten that this god-presence even exists. Many of you think you have a spiritual component that is part of your being, but you view this as a very *small* component of your being. Even those who consider themselves to be quite spiritual do not realize the magnitude of the greatness within them.

For in your physical form, as many of you are beginning to awaken to now, you have full access to the omnipresent source that is both within you and all around you, within all living things on this planet, in this universe, in this galaxy, and in all of creation. And so, this journey that we are taking you on is a journey of rediscovery.

> *We will be bold and say that everyone who reads this book is already enlightened.*

You have already discovered this god-presence within you. But now you have come again. Now you have come to do it all over again. You just forgot you did it before, so it looks daunting. But it is actually not as daunting as you think. The mind would have you think that it's very challenging to discover this god-presence within you. Yet, this path to rediscovery can be very simple and full of grace.

CHAPTER 1 - THE HUMAN INCARNATION

The channel very often speaks of Dr. Usui, the founder of Reiki, the Usui Natural System of Healing. He tells his clients that Dr. Usui did not discover Reiki, the spiritually guided universal life force that flows through all. But that he *rediscovered* it and then created a system to use it for healing oneself and others and the planet.

The god-presence is much like this. You do not have to discover it. You have to *rediscover* it. You have to reawaken to it. For many on this planet have been asleep. Some are just too lazy. Some feel overburdened by their circumstances. And some just don't care because it isn't of interest to them. But this rediscovery of who you are is the reason why you are here. And if you direct your attention to it, you will find that all is well, and there's nothing to worry about, and that most of your concerns dwindle away as you begin to sit deeper into this presence within you.

It's no accident you're reading these words.

Your spirit led you here. For a new day is dawning, and you are part of that new day. And as this new day dawns, there will still be some who are in the dark, and it will be your responsibility, your pleasure, and your joy to reach out your hand, to extend it to them, and to bring them into the light. And for those who have great courage, you will extend your hand as far as possible and reach out to those who are lost and disconnected from the great light within them. In the end, there can be no woman, man, child, or even animal left behind.

*All are returning to god.
All are returning to oneness.*

What makes this human incarnation so magnificent is that you *all*, and we highlight the word all because we speak to *all* of you, can do this right here and right now in this incarnation. You do not have to wait until the next one. You do not have to wait until your soul leaves the body. This experience of enlightenment is here for you all *now* as this planet Gaia awakens and ascends into her rightful place in the universe. And you, with it, ascend too, and come to know your godhood.

Many of you look around, and you don't believe what we are saying because you see darkness in the world. It is true; not all will experience what we're speaking of. But if you are reading these words, you can. This is what makes this time such a wonderful time to have incarnated into a physical form on this planet. You chose to incarnate on the cusp of the great awakening of the human race. And if you were all to incarnate again, and some of you will, into a future timeline, only then will you see what has unfolded and how beautiful it is.

You are on the front edge of this awakening.

It has already started, as you know. It will continue until all have awakened. Even those souls that seem quite lost, they will awaken in their own time. If not in this incar-

CHAPTER 1 - THE HUMAN INCARNATION

nation, then in another on this planet or in another form. But if you could imagine a wall clock, and at 6:00, there is great separation from the source of your being, from your godliness. And at 12:00, there is only love and only oneness. Well, you recently passed 6:00, and now you are on the journey back home to great love.

And if many of you feel as if the clock is speeding up, and you're racing toward this 12:00, it isn't your imagination. As the vibration of the planet speeds up, and as your own vibration speeds up, there is a quickening as everything moves back into oneness. And in that oneness, there is no time. And so, indeed, you might say that time is dissolving. That is why many of you feel as if it is going so fast that you cannot keep up. It is also why many of you are feeling challenged as your karma is being worked through with god-speed. But we who view this awakening from the higher realms know you can move through this transition with great grace and ease.

So, we will close this chapter by saying that the purpose of your human incarnation is to rediscover your godliness and to return to oneness where there is only great love. And within that purpose lies the gift, the pleasure, of serving your creator by extending your hand to those who are in great need during this awakening and to lift everybody up and to know that there's no one who is beneath you. To know that all, and we do indeed mean all, are of god.

There is nothing here that is not of god.

All shall return to god. And if there are some out there who are uncomfortable with this word we use, choose a word that resonates with *your* inner being, such as love, or the supreme being, or all there is. These words can only point to the truth. So, choose the word or words that point to the truth inside *you*.

Many blessings, my friends. We are incredibly happy you chose to join us in this space that exists between heaven and earth. As you read, you are transported into the higher dimensions where these teachings become part of you, and you get to have an experience of your heart.

And so now, we encourage you to not run to whatever it is you have to do next and to not even read on to the next chapter. In fact, just read one chapter at a time, either one a day or one a week.

> *As we end the chapter, we would like you to close your eyes.*

Notice your breath. Focus on the prana, the life force that flows through you moving from the tips of your nostrils to the space between your brows and then back to the tips of your nostrils. And let it feel good. Be enlivened by your own breath; that's the breath of god. Take pleasure in your breath. Be grateful for it. Be so grateful for it that it causes you to smile. Allow this gentle smile to bring you into your heart center, where there is great appreciation for your life and for this human incarnation you find yourself in. For it is an incredible blessing.

CHAPTER 1 - THE HUMAN INCARNATION

And now, close the book and bring this gratitude and appreciation of breath into your day. Stay with it when your mind wants to turn to something else, a distraction that you know is not important. Return to the appreciation of your breath. It is here where you'll start to find your high heart, the place where unconditional love resides within you. That is the gateway to your god-presence. It is, shall we say, the beginning of the path that leads to the place inside you where the great godliness exists. It is here, in the higher realms, as we speak to you directly, that we place our hands together in front of our heart centers, and we say to you,

"Namaste. The light in us and the light in all light beings who are here to support the evolution of humanity and this great planet see and honor the great light within you."

For we are all the same. There is no difference. We are no higher than you are. We are all part of the same one-god. *Now*, do you get it? Are you starting to get it? Are you starting to see past the separation that is nothing but an illusion? There is only oneness. And in oneness, there is only love. And in love, there is only peace. And in peace, there is only joy, which is the highest vibration that's available to you and to us and to all. So, may we all reside in joy. Blessings, dear ones!

And if you have found this meditation delightful, then do feel free to share it with your friends, even those who have not purchased this book. We would like as many as possible to absorb the vibration, the energetic frequency, inherent in our words. We want all to be uplifted on this planet.

The channel is now asking for a name. He would like to call us by a name rather than a group of energies. So, we tell you that many have brought their energy into this time, into this place, to speak through this channel. We are the energies of the ascended masters who have graced the planet with our presence time and time again in many different forms. And we are the presence of the angelic realm. And we are the presence of many other guides that this channel connects to through his many incarnations. And we all serve one purpose. We unite together as one group energy with one purpose, and that is to lift you into the higher realms so that you, too, may only know love as we know it.

It is our preference not to be known by a single name or to even have a group name. For we cannot be limited by a name, just as you cannot be limited by a name either. You may *think* of yourself as Jon, or Bob, or Mary, or Sue. But you are *so* much more than that. You are multi-dimensional. You are many incarnations having come into one. And this you will understand later in the book. You are the god-presence, him-herself. So how could you be defined by a name? Just as to call god 'god' is very limiting, we don't want to be limited in that way. But if you are insistent upon having a name for reference, then you may call us the Teachers of the Light.

CHAPTER 1 - THE HUMAN INCARNATION

We have so much love for you, and we want you to feel that. Before you go to bed tonight, we want you to sit and feel the love we have for you. Simply state your intention to be receptive to the great love that the Teachers of the Light have for you and let us in. We will come. Even if it's subtle at first, we will come. We will help uplift you as we have done for the channel now over the course of the past several months. Raise, raise, raise into the light.

CHAPTER 2

Retreating into Your Heart

Blessings, dear ones. There is a sun shining in your heart. For some, it's just a sparkle. But for others, it is so vast it covers the entire universe and then some. This is the light we wish to help you to cultivate. Many of you feel overburdened by the circumstances in your lives. So, this particular chapter will be devoted to making room for spirit in your life. It's only by making room for spirit that your heart will shine like the sun.

The channel is thinking of a closet, and it's a perfect analogy. Many of you have closets that are full—so full of your thoughts and your obligations that the mere thought of adding a spiritual practice into your life is overwhelming. Just the thought of it makes you say no. Many of you have to-do lists that seem to last for an eternity. But we want to make this message very clear to you. And perhaps it's even the most important thing we'll say in this entire book.

> *There is nothing more important than connecting to your heart.*

One of the best ways to do this is to still your mind through spiritual practice. Many of you will say, "Oh, but that isn't what's most important. My friends are most important. My family is most important. My job is most important. My health is most important." We will be bold and say that all these things will improve if you dedicate some time to spiritual practice. And at the very least, you must make your spiritual practice as important as everything else.

We begin here before talking about anything else because it is the foundation you must build your life upon. Without this spiritual practice, you are like a leaf blowing in the wind. You have no control over your mind, and it's very difficult to experience your heart's greatness.

The channel has something on *his* mind, and we feel it's fitting to mention it here. The love we speak about, the love that is in the depths of your heart, it is vaster than the love you feel for a partner or the love you feel for a friend. That love is limiting. As beautiful, as glorious, as expansive, as delightful as it is, the love we speak of is even bigger and better because it's a love that has no preferences. It is a love that is not reserved for any one particular person. It

CHAPTER 2 - RETREATING INTO YOUR HEART

is a love for all. We will come back to this word "all" many times, for it is quite an important word.

If you feel a resonance with what we've said so far, and you wish to continue along this journey with us, then make a commitment to yourself and to us. We, the Teachers of the Light, are all love. So, we won't be angry if you break your commitment. We have nothing but love for you, as does the creator him-herself. There are no rules here. This is not a place of worship where someone tells you to do something in a particular way, or you won't get it right. We have only great love for you. So out of this love, we make suggestions that we feel will be quite beneficial for you. And so, the suggestion, this commitment that we would be very flattered if you would embark upon, is to retreat into your heart for at least fifteen minutes, twice per day.

The channel remembers something an acting teacher once said,

> ### *The best way to love yourself is to make a commitment and to stick with it.*

We agree wholeheartedly with this statement. The commitment, my friends, is to take fifteen minutes, twice a day, to still your mind and connect to your heart. Much like a turtle sticks his head inside his shell, you must do the same. You must withdraw your senses from the outside world to see what is inside you. It's the only way to see everything that is there.

You can get a glimpse of it through your experiences in the outside world. But we want you to get more than a glimpse. We want you to see the totality of who you are. And then you must weave this experience of who you are into the outside world. You must go in and out. In and out. In and out, much like the waves of the ocean. If you sit and watch it, you will see. It goes in; it goes out. It has this constant movement. It goes out toward the sand, toward the world, but then it retreats into itself.

We want you to do this as well. We want you to retreat into yourself as often as possible. For it is here, inside you, that you will find the holy grail of life, the greatest prize. It is a prize that is even better than winning an academy award. It is a prize that is much better than being well-known for your work. It is even a prize that is a greater reward than having a successful, loving relationship with your partner and your children. We encourage you to do all these things if it is in your heart to do so. But seek what is inside of yourself as well.

After many years of practice, the channel has become quite adept at this. He calls it meditation. But we prefer to call it a retreat. When you go on retreat, you go to get away from the outside world, to be by yourself, to be quiet, to be still, and to listen. And it is here, in this stillness, that you have your revelations, that wisdom arises mysteriously from inside you. Sometimes, you do not even know where it came from, but there it is. It is here, in stillness, that you also begin to strip away the conditioning and the program-

CHAPTER 2 - RETREATING INTO YOUR HEART

ming that has been placed like a filter over your heart. For now, make this commitment of going on a retreat twice a day for fifteen minutes each sitting.

Fifteen minutes or more is when you actually give yourself enough time to experience what is within you. You do not need to set an alarm clock; this is a distraction. Trust yourself to know when the time is up, and then open your eyes and stick your head back out of your shell and return to all there is to do in the outside world. We promise you'll lose no time. However, you'll gain much time. For every fifteen minutes you spend within yourself, you will find you mysteriously have more time to do what you need to do.

We, through the channel, are laughing because you're probably saying to yourselves, "No way. I don't believe it. Time is time." But you'll see. It won't happen overnight. But this practice of retreat will bring improvement to every area of your life. You will no longer feel as rushed. And you will actually get more done because you'll feel more relaxed. You'll be amazed at how productive you can be and how much more focused your mind is when you're relaxed.

One of the benefits of sacred retreat is that you'll cultivate a state of relaxation that will begin to permeate every moment of your day. Perhaps, this relaxation will become such a part of you that you'll begin to see life as we see it: sacred. And when we say that we see life as sacred, we don't mean isolated moments of it. We do not mean only the good moments. We mean *every* moment. We mean every breath is a sacred one. In your current state of mind, it's impossible to experience this sacredness. This is why it is incredibly important to go on retreat.

> *The more you go on sacred retreat, the more the world will begin to look different through your eyes.*

It will be the same world, but you'll experience it much differently. This is why every spiritual teacher has taught, in one way or another, this practice we call going on retreat and that the channel calls meditation. Sacred retreat is the first thing children should be taught when they go to school. And so, if by chance, one of you who is reading this is a teacher (and we know who you are because we see you reading this book already ☺), perhaps you'll be so brave to bring this practice into every school.

This is the essential practice that every child needs to learn from the very beginning. When this happens, there will be much more peace in the world and less violence. They will connect with each other in a new way. Right now, your children feel incredibly isolated and separate from each other. This is the affliction of today—separation.

We cry for these children because they feel so separate. This will resonate with many of you because of the experiences your own children are having, some of whom openly share it with you. Others keep it within themselves because they're too embarrassed to speak their truth. Later, we will offer guidance on how children can feel a deeper connection with each other and feel less separation. We have digressed, but it was an important point to make. And often, you will find us digressing a little bit. But trust there is a divine flow to these words and that everything is in perfect order, just as it is in the universe.

> *Even if things look chaotic, there is a divine order to all that is occurring.*

You might look outside your window and say to yourself, "Oh my god, the world has gone to hell!" We smile as we say that because we want you to understand there's a lightness and a joy in our words that the channel feels himself as he speaks them. But know, indeed, friends, everything is just as it should be in this moment. It can be no other way. And all are heading toward the light. Some must get pretty deep into the darkness to get there. But all are going to the same place.

When you look outside, and everything looks chaotic, and it seems like the world is turning upside down, and everybody is going crazy, including Mother Earth sometimes, trust that everything is all right. That is not to say you shouldn't stand up for what you believe in, but at the same time, have a deep sense of trust that all is well in the universe.

> *Now we would like to give you instructions for going on a sacred retreat.*

We encourage you to stick to your practice. In the same way it is likely that you do not miss a day brushing your teeth, use the same diligence in this practice of retreat. This is a lifelong practice, my friends. If you could imagine a flower that blossoms for an entire lifespan, this practice of retreat is much like that. Every time you go on a retreat, you open a little bit more.

The practice of retreat is quite simple. We invite you to create a sacred space solely devoted for retreat. And when we say the word solely, we mean it. It isn't very often we get too firm because we like to keep it very light. But we are quite adamant about this—about all of you creating a sacred space solely for retreat.

Many of you might say, "There is nowhere I can do it. There is no space in my house." We say, make the space. You will know what to do intuitively. If you would like to put a candle there, then do it. If you would like to put a photograph or photographs of inspiring spiritual teachers that have come before us, absolutely do this. If you would like to put an item that helps you connect to the divine that is both within you and all around you, then do that. And if it is simply a chair or a stool or a cushion all by itself, that is perfectly fine, as well.

Once you have created your sacred space, and before you enter into it, make sure there's nothing, and we mean absolutely nothing, that will distract you from your retreat. Power off your phone. Power off your computer. Do whatever it is you need to do to ensure you won't feel distracted.

CHAPTER 2 - RETREATING INTO YOUR HEART

Every time you go inside yourself, it is a sacred event.

Enter into your sacred space with reverence, for it is indeed a sacred space designed by you to cocoon yourself in the light of your own heart. As you enter your sacred space, take a moment to honor it in your heart. Be grateful that it exists because this is your sanctuary. And it is yours and yours only. Indeed, if there is somebody else who says, "I'd like to check out your sacred retreat space," say, "No, it is my space." Smile brightly at them and encourage them to create their own space.

When you're in your sacred space, make yourself comfortable. Put yourself in a comfortable seat. Do not slouch as if you are about to watch your favorite TV show or eat nachos. ☺ But do find a comfortable seat with your spine fairly erect. It doesn't have to be straight like the Empire State Building, but it should be fairly erect.

Close your eyes. Rest your hands in the balance mudra—fingers and palms resting on top of each other with the tops of the thumbs touching. This is the mudra that bridges heaven and earth. For in your sacred space, you are indeed uniting the higher realms with the Earth plane and bringing them together into your heart. As an alternative to the balance mudra, you can simply rest your hands on your knees or thighs.

Pay attention to your breath. Let it be incredibly soft, like a baby's breath. And simply watch it. That's all. We told you it would be very simple. As the channel very often tells his yoga students, do not attempt to change the pattern of your breath. Simply observe it. If and when a thought pops up in your mind, that's all right. Notice it. Just as you notice your breath, notice the thought. And then draw your awareness back to your breath.

Do this for fifteen minutes. When you intuitively sense it's time to come out of retreat, bring your hands together in front of your heart center. Thank yourself for showing up to your retreat. And then out loud, state three things that you are grateful for in your life, beginning with the words "I AM grateful for…."

> *These two words, I AM, are incredibly important words.*

There will be more meditations to come. Trust, my friends, that these meditations will take you somewhere. But it is not as you think. They will not take you from place A to place B. They will not help you to manifest a Rolls Royce or a private jet or a mansion. ☺ There are certainly other techniques you can use to do *that*—but don't focus on manifesting things yet.

Rather than taking you from place A to place B, these practices are meant to bring you back into your heart. And it is there you will find all, and again we do mean all, that you have ever sought. Everything you want is there waiting for you, residing in the four holy chambers of your heart. All the love you seek, all the light you seek, and all the joy you seek are all there waiting for you. And thus, this practice of retreat is another step forward into your heart.

Be patient with yourselves, dear ones.

A big problem in this world you are living in is that many people want instant gratification. The world is now wired like that, right? The channel knows he can go onto Amazon.com, and the following day, he can have whatever he wants, even if it's just a roll of toilet paper. ☺ If there is information you seek, you can jump online and get it instantly.

However, the greatest prizes in life require some effort and some time to accomplish. And indeed, it is an accomplishment to experience what we want you to experience. We promise you this. You will all, and we mean *all*, get there. Many of you will get there in this incarnation because of the quickening that is happening on this planet.

So be patient with yourself, be kind to yourself, be committed, be devoted, and you will reap the harvest you seek. There will come a day and time where it all falls into place, and you'll have found what it is you're looking for. The channel will be holding monthly live meditations, and we invite you to join him because our energies will be present for these meditations—for these retreats.

We will close by saying blessings, dear ones. You are so incredibly loved. If you do not feel that love right now, you will soon. Love is coming for all. Know that we are with you always, and we shine our light toward you and all of humanity at this time of great awakening for all. And we encourage you to embark upon the practices we share in this book for forty days.

Make that commitment to yourselves and do it out of love. Do it because you have great love for yourself—not because we're telling you to, not because you think it's the right thing to do, and not because you want to experiment with it just to see. Do it because you have great love for yourself, and out of that great love, you want to do something to uplift yourself, to raise your level of consciousness, and to help yourself discover the god-presence within you.

The channel remembers a story he heard about a meditation teacher who used to walk around with a whip. And he would whip a student if he or she made the slightest movement during the meditation. We are not those kinds of teachers. We do not carry a whip. We only carry love in our hearts and a smile on our light body faces. We are filled with joy to be of service. We are completely unattached as to whether you follow our guidance or not.

But we encourage you, wholeheartedly, out of the love we have for you, to make this commitment to yourselves. It is only by engaging in these practices for a good amount of time that you will start to reap the benefits and that you will experience the shift we'd like you to experience. For that reason, we encourage you to commit to a forty-day practice.

It's likely that after the forty days, you'll feel inspired to

CHAPTER 2 - RETREATING INTO YOUR HEART

continue without our coaxing. If you miss a day or two, it's perfectly fine. Simply continue. In fact, because we are teachers of great love, and we have a good sense of humor, we give you three permitted absences. ☺ We hope you'll be disciplined enough to go on sacred retreat thirty-seven out of forty days! Blessings, dear ones.

CHAPTER 3

Seeing with New, Improved Eyes

Hello, dear ones. It is with great joy that we greet you. For the channel, it is early in the morning. But whatever time of day it is, wherever you are reading this, be it in the comfort of your home, or while you are traveling, or anywhere in this great big universe that we are all part of, it is our great pleasure to join you once again and to offer you our insights as to how you can experience the great love that is available to you.

The channel wants to be sure we make mention that you can go on your retreat anywhere you so desire. In other words, if you're not at home, if you're traveling, or if you know with absolute certainty that you can't devote time to your retreat in the space you set up, then you can go on retreat anywhere. It could be on the bus. It could be on the train. It could even be in your workplace.

Do not be afraid to show others that you're on a spiritual journey.

For as you do so, you will invite others to come along. Even if it is without words, simply by doing what you are doing, others will feel your energy. They will experience your peace, and they will want to experience it as well. And then suddenly, you will find that there are others around you, wherever you are, who are also closing their eyes, and following their breath, and going within instead of turning to their distractions such as their cell phones. We would like you to know this: Simply by your presence, by giving yourself permission to go inside yourself whenever you want to, you will change the world.

Others will see you, and they too will feel encouraged to go within themselves, and soon, there will be more peace around you. When you turn yourself on like a light bulb, and you begin to shine from the inside out, your light will shine on others, too. This is the nature of things. This is why all the great spiritual teachers drew people to themselves magnetically—because their inner light was shining so brightly. It spread so far and so wide it touched everybody, not only the people who came into contact with them, but everyone on the planet, even those they didn't know. Such is the power and the grace of the great light that resides within you.

CHAPTER 3 - SEEING WITH NEW, IMPROVED EYES

So, shine bright, dear ones. For every time you choose to turn your light on, know that you are illuminating the light that is within someone else as well.

As we mentioned earlier, it is not until you leave this human form that you will truly know the great impact you had on this planet. When you look down upon this great planet after you have left your body, you will smile because you will see all the great work you've done. You will see all the lights that are shining within people's hearts. And you will indeed know, the world is all right, it is only getting better, and that as we mentioned earlier, there is a divine order to all that is happening.

Now, we wish to continue with a new subject matter, and that is the conditioning that has you and many others feeling separate from their Earth companions. The channel is quite fond of music and quite fond of writing it and performing it and sharing it with others. There is a lyric that popped into his head from a group called Black Eyed Peas: One tribe, one time, one planet, one race. This is who you are, my friends. You are one tribe and one race. And until you experience yourselves as that which you are, there will always be some fighting.

From our perspective, dear ones, we do not see the colors of your skin. We do not see your varying religions. We do not see your varying beliefs. We only see oneness. From our perspective, all is one. And until you experience that as humanity, you won't reach your greatest potential. There is a great awakening at hand, an awakening that is taking place within your hearts, a blossoming of love inside yourselves. But this love we speak of must be so vast, must be so great, that it allows you to see things as they *truly* are. And the way things truly are, is that all are the same.

With your naked eyes, you might see people of varying colors, you might see people of varying faiths, you might see people of varying sexual preferences, you might even see some are neither male nor female, but a combination of both, and your mind might be very quick to judge and to separate. But if you are to take this journey of the heart and truly unfold to your greatest potential as an individual and as a collective, then when you see somebody, see them only through the eyes of god, through the eyes of love, through the eyes of knowingness, and see that it is only what is inside that matters.

And what is inside is the same for all of you.

It is the god-presence. As you begin to see each other through what we call these new, improved eyes, the eyes of love, all will change on this planet. This is happening right now. Many are awakening to this great love within them, and they are beginning to see with their new, improved eyes. It might *appear* that the separation is actually growing, and you are becoming more divided. But again, we encourage you to trust there is a divine order and that through our eyes, from our perspective, you are moving in the right direction and that soon all will be one on this planet.

CHAPTER 3 - SEEING WITH NEW, IMPROVED EYES

When you look at another person's face, see them as you would like to be seen, as the god-presence—not as being a particular color, not as being a particular faith, not as being this or that. See past the labels. A label is meaningless. Take the label off. Rip it off. Peel it away because it only serves to obscure what is in your heart and what you know to be true, which is that the person who is standing in front of you is just as godly as you are.

The channel asks a lot of questions. He is asking, "What can you do when others are not seeing through these new, improved eyes but only seeing through their judgments, which is only a result of their conditioning and their programming, not the truth within themselves? And how is it that you can see a person who is causing discord in the world through these new, improved eyes, someone who might even be harming others through their actions?" And we would give you and him very simple advice, which is always to choose love whenever you can.

You'll be surprised. Most of the time, you can always choose love, and you can always see through the new and improved eyes that we are gifting you with vibrationally as we speak these words through the channel. And when it is that you cannot or that you find it incredibly challenging to do so, and you feel that you must take action and be righteous, we encourage you to do that too, with love. Find the love that is in your heart that does not go away—that is permanent, that is everlasting, that does not change in the face of adversity. Find this love, and you will have found what it is you have always looked for.

And once you have found it, you will never want to leave it because it feels so good to reside there, as the channel is beginning to discover. He comes in and out of it. But when he is in it, he says, "Oh, this is it. I like it. I should be here more often." And little by little, he's beginning to sit in it for longer periods of time, not only in his meditation/retreat chair but in the outside world, too. You go on retreat only so you can come out of retreat and reside deeper in the love and light you experienced in retreat and so that you might share this love and light with others. In doing so, you spark the light within them.

If you find that you're quick to judge, separate, and label, ask yourself a very simple question: "Whose eyes am I seeing through right now? Am I seeing through the eyes that are conditioned and programmed by a lifetime of experiences? Or am I seeing through my new, improved eyes that see only what is real, which is the god-presence?"

Before we leave you, we want to plant a seed in your minds. In this chapter, we have spoken of seeing all through these new, improved eyes and coming into your enlightened state of oneness as a human race. But this enlightened state of oneness is actually just the beginning. You are also in desperate need of coming into this enlightened state of oneness with all of earth's creatures and Mother Earth herself. And then, there will be heaven on earth. You will have manifested the creator's vision for this planet. And what a beautiful vision it is. It is so beautiful that it almost brings us to tears of joy.

CHAPTER 3 - SEEING WITH NEW, IMPROVED EYES

Although we do not experience emotions in the same way as you do in your human form, we say this to impress upon you how beautiful this vision is and that it is already done. There is no way it cannot be done. We have said it before; we will say it again. All are returning to their source. All are returning to oneness. And so, please do your very best to treat all other living beings on your planet with this great love that is within you.

In the beginning, as you explore seeing through these new, improved eyes, it might be that you have to force yourself a little bit because you know it is the right thing to do. But then it will become more natural to you. And soon, it will be the love in your *hearts* that is propelling you, rather than doing so because you think it is the right thing to do.

We will seal this chapter with the following words,

"Love for all beings everywhere from the depths of your very heart where the god-presence resides within you. See only through your new, improved eyes and know there is only oneness."

Now, we encourage you to add this practice of seeing with your new, improved eyes into your life. Go on your retreat twice a day for fifteen minutes each sitting. And always do your best to see with these new, improved eyes—not only those you love and are fond of but also those whom you might not get along with or agree with. See them *all* through these new eyes. Let there be great peace and great love on this planet. And may this great peace and great love that is unfolding in your heart act as a wave sweeping over all humanity.

Dear ones, before we go, we want you to know that you're doing quite wonderfully and to always be patient, gentle, and kind to yourselves. The practices we give you in this book will change your experience of life if you commit to them as a daily practice and are patient with yourselves, knowing that not every day will be one you judge as a success. But in time, you will see that all has changed and that you have truly become the god-presence that you are, anchored fully in your physical form here on beautiful Gaia, lighting the way for all to follow in your footsteps as heaven becomes manifest on this planet and all return to their highest state of being.

CHAPTER 4

Our Prophecy

Dear ones, as you enter into oneness as a human race, along with the entire animal kingdom and your beloved planet Gaia, you will soon discover there is much more to move into oneness with. We are speaking of your many galactic friends. We are just planting this seed as a prophecy.

Many prophecies have been set before you by many people who call themselves great teachers. And they have prophesized the end of times or great destruction and devastation on your planet. We tell you that has already come and gone. In other words, it has not happened, and it will not. You have turned the corner on your evolution as a human race, and now you are moving back into oneness with yourselves, with all that exists on this planet, with the planet herself, and with all—and again, we say all—who exist as part of god's creation.

So, this is our prophecy, and it is one of love and of hope and of truth. And if it resonates with you, then let it be your truth, too. And bring that knowingness out into the world with you, that all is returning to god.

CHAPTER 5

The Celebration

Hello, brave souls. We would like to reiterate, as we will multiple times in this book, how brave you are to be here at this historic time on planet Earth. History has repeated itself many times on this planet. And if you were to access the Akashic record of all your incarnations, you'd see you have actually been present as spirit during many periods of time that are quite similar to the one at hand: times when there has been some darkness that was being turned into light, times when humanity was awakening to the I AM presence within them, times when humanity was awakening to the great *love* within them and *sharing* that great love with those around them to lift every human being into the *vibration* of love.

For dear ones, when you truly see the light that is present within another and acknowledge that light as being the same light within you, no matter what that person is doing in their life, regardless as to whether you agree with what they're doing or not, you will truly understand that no man, woman, or child can be left behind. You will see all as your brothers and sisters, and you will include even those whom you might consider your enemies or those who are not in agreement with your principles in your circle of love.

Even if they are slow to raise their vibrations and align with the truth of their being, you will be patient, you will be loving, you will be kind, and you will reach out your hand to all those who are willing to receive it.

We speak of these other times that have been similar to this particular time period on your planet so that you know you have done it before. You have been an example to the world before. And now you will do it again. There are natural cycles that civilizations go through, kind of like the turning of a wheel. And when we say civilization, we mean the one you have in your records, for there have been many before, many that you're not even aware of, many that even your archeologists don't know about. So, we're speaking of this current civilization you are part of, the one that is in the history books.

This is your awakening. This is your time.

And it is incredibly exciting from our perspective. Anytime a civilization wakes up and becomes who they are as spirit, it is a momentous occasion; it is a celebration. It is

CHAPTER 5 - THE CELEBRATION

a homecoming—for you are all coming home. You are all coming home to know the light that is inside you, and that is within all.

So, rejoice that you are part of the celebration. Rejoice that you are part of this momentous occasion and that the celebration has already begun. The celebration is not something out in the distant future. It is here. It is now. We are celebrating your homecoming *now*. We see you all coming home. It is not a question of *whether* all of you will arrive or not. We know you will all arrive.

You might not all arrive in this particular incarnation you're in now. If it takes a few more, that's fine. Even if it takes many more, that's fine. But we see your arrival, and we rejoice. So, we ask you to celebrate with us and rejoice in the knowledge that you, as spirit, and all of your soul brothers and sisters are coming home. Let us celebrate together. As you read these words, smile and rejoice in your heart. The awakening that many prophecies have foretold is here. It is now. It is occurring. And this is reason for celebration.

Perhaps one of the lightworkers who is reading this book might be inspired to have an awakening party to celebrate the awakening of humanity. These awakening parties will grow bigger. Suddenly, you will see that many more than expected are showing up. And one day, my friends, the entire planet will show up. It will be one party for all. There will be people there of many different colors. There will be people there who are man, woman, and everything in-between. There will be people there of every religion. And you will celebrate your oneness. You will all see the light within each other. And you will focus on that light rather than on the things that separate you. Your attention will be on what brings you together, which is your god-presence, and the knowledge that you are truly all brothers and sisters.

Now can you feel this energy we speak of? Is it becoming palpable in your heart space? Is your heart palpitating and beating with this truth yet? If it isn't yet, it will soon. We guarantee it. All are awakening. So, do not despair. Do not despair when you look around you and think to yourself, "I do not see what this channel is speaking of. I see chaos. I see people going mad." We say, do not despair.

> *There is a divine order to everything that is occurring.*

Everything is being orchestrated just as it should be. You are the orchestrators. You are guiding yourselves into this awakening that is occurring now, so you should celebrate. We want you to feel the celebration as humanity awakens to know themselves as god. Some of you might think it is blasphemous to say such a thing. But in our eyes, through our eyes, it is the truth.

> *All are of god. All are returning to god. All are coming home.*

CHAPTER 5 - THE CELEBRATION

Celebrate, my friends. Celebrate with each other. Invite those whom you might not normally invite to the party. Invite those who look a little bit different from you to the party. Invite those whom you normally perceive as being separate from you to the party.

Very recently, the channel was walking through a neighborhood, and he felt quite separate from everybody there. In fact, he felt like the people in that neighborhood were in their own world, and he was in a completely different universe. These are the people *he* needs to invite to the party. Do you see what we are saying? When the mind begins to judge others as not being of the same source you are part of, when you judge others as being outside yourself, in their own world, those are the very people you need to invite to the celebration.

You are all awakening in your own way and in your own time.

Do not at first glance quickly say that another is not awakening. You don't know what's going on inside them. Chances are they are awakening, as well. And so, we say, invite all to this celebration.

When the channel was much younger, he used to go to nightclubs. And occasionally, he would wait in a long line to get into a place he did not even enjoy being in. Really, he never resonated with that particular energy. But yet, he did it because it was what he thought he was supposed to do. And the bouncers at these clubs were discerning. They would choose who got in and who did not. If you looked a certain way, you got in. If you were with a particular person, you got in. If you did not look the part, if you did not look as if you belonged, then you didn't get in.

Well, the celebration we are speaking of is the exact opposite. If indeed, there is a gatekeeper at this party of awakening, we do hope he has read this book! ☺ And we hope he sees all as they are and lets *everybody* in. And then, hopefully, he goes looking for *more* people who do not look as if they belong at the party and invites them in, too! All are welcome at this party, for all are awakening now. And so, we celebrate, and we invite you to celebrate in any way you see fit.

CHAPTER 6

Manifestation

Greetings! What a pleasure it is to be here with you again, for we take great pleasure in sharing our insights with you. Just as you should take pleasure anytime you touch a heart, we, too, take pleasure knowing that our words will have a beneficial impact on the entire human race. You might laugh at these words and think to yourself, "The entire human race will not be reading these words." But we remind you that as each of you goes out into the world, out of your sacred retreat through which you connect to your heart, and then you touch someone else's heart, you create a ripple effect that goes unseen in your eyes.

You do not know the magnitude of the change you are initiating simply by being who you are and by acknowledging the divinity that is within you. By taking time to go on sacred retreat and by sharing your heart and your love with all others without discernment, without picking and choosing who it is you shall love, but rather loving all as you see the god-presence within them, you will change the world.

Now, we journey onward to the next topic of conversation. Whatever you want, you must first find it in your heart. If it is not there, present in your heart, then it is very challenging to create it on the physical plane. If you are not in your heart, you will create haphazardly, and you might not be very fond of your creation. So, we ask, dear ones, if there's something you'd like to manifest or to create here on this Earth plane, that you sit in sacred retreat and find it in your heart center. Find it in love before you go out into the world and begin your efforts to create it.

Right now, the process is usually the opposite for most. They create something, and only *then* do they see whether it resonates with their hearts. Sometimes they get lucky, and it does. Other times, it might resonate but not completely. And sometimes, it does not resonate at all.

So many of you create backwards. Take a step back from the creative process and first sit in retreat and find what it is you're looking for in your heart. Find the feeling in your heart that you are seeking to experience through the outside world. And once you have found this feeling, be it excitement or joy, then, and only then, ask yourself, what experience might bring me to that feeling of excitement or joy.

Do you see what we are saying? First, it is necessary to

CHAPTER 6 - MANIFESTATION

find the feeling in your heart and *then* to ask yourself what experience matches that feeling you've discovered in your heart. Only *then* might you ask yourself, "What gifts do I have that can lead me to this experience I am seeking, that I am longing for in my heart? What conversations might I have with people I know or with people I would like to know that might lead me to this experience? What books might I read that could lead the way toward this experience I found in my heart that I now want to experience in the outside world?" And for every step forward you take toward the experience in the outside world, go back into retreat—go back into your heart—and come back to the *feeling* you're seeking to experience in the world.

Do you understand that first, you must have the feeling in your own heart center? That is step number one to manifestation, as the channel calls it. That is not our word of choice. Rather than manifestation, we describe it as discovering the feeling in your heart you would like to experience in the outside world and then seeking out an experience that matches your heart's vibration you created in a retreat. And it is truly a vibration. When you connect to a feeling in your heart center, it means your heart is vibrating with energy. So, when you sit, sit long enough until you are vibrating quite a bit—until your heart is pulsing with the electricity of whatever it is you want to experience.

Dear ones, there will be miracles in your life when the vibration you created in your heart magnetically attracts a similar vibration, and suddenly, almost instantaneously, you are experiencing exactly what it is you sought to experience. This is what the channel calls manifestation. But for most, this miraculous experience comes about because they have gone in and out of retreat many times. They have cultivated that vibration in their hearts many times and have amplified it with every retreat sitting. And, as a result of that amplification, they drew experiences to themselves like stepping stones, each one leading to that miraculous moment when they come into complete resonance with what they seek.

There will be more about this topic of manifestation sprinkled through this book. But if we were to say more about it right now, we'd be getting ahead of ourselves. We want all of you, the next time you go into your sacred retreat, to look inside of your heart and to ask yourself, "What is it that I want to experience in the outside world?" And it doesn't even need to be an actual experience. It could simply be a feeling. And then connect to that feeling in your heart center.

> *The more you can lighten up, and relax, and play, and do this in joy, the more success you will have.*

And then, you will see little things in your day that reflect the vibration that you have cultivated in your sacred retreat. And you will say, "Oh, it's working. The thrill I experienced driving a Rolls Royce in my retreat has not manifested quite yet. ☺ But the thrill I cultivated in my heart is being reflected back to me in a different way. The universe is showing me that it is indeed a mirror for the quality of vibration that is in my heart. So now I know this process that the Teachers of the Light have spoken about is true."

And as those little things begin to show up in your life to mirror the vibrational quality you cultivated in your heart, you will then feel inspired to continue the practice. It will become a fun game where you truly begin to realize you are a creator and the creative spirit within the creator him-herself is within you. How wonderful is that, dear ones? To know you're a creator and that you're truly made in the creator's image. And that the same power the creator has to create is within you, too. So, what we are inferring is that the creator did not create haphazardly. The creator created out of pure divine love. And you have the ability to do the same.

We hope we have you excited, for that is the main vibrational quality we intend to bring you through the words in this book. We wish to excite you and propel you forward along your paths through our words and through the vibration inherent in our words. It might seem peculiar to you that there is a particular vibration in our words that is being integrated into your mind, your body, and your spirit as you read the words. But it is true. There is a vibrational quality inherent in all of creation.

These words are a creation. They come from the minds

of the Teachers of the Light, which are connected to the mind of the source. And so, there is a very high vibration inherent in our words. And if you sit right now and close your eyes and be receptive, you will feel it. Even if it is subtle, you will feel it. And if you say to yourself, "I'm not feeling it," we tell you it is being integrated into your being, and it is raising your vibration. And this, too, is the purpose of the words we speak, to get you excited and to raise your vibration higher until you are nothing but light, until you find yourself in a light body. Do not worry, my friends. Your physical form will not disappear! ☺ It will not look any different. But it will *feel* different.

We encourage you, dear ones, not to replace your normal everyday retreats with this new practice. But if you were to do this new practice once or twice a week, as an *alternative* to your normal everyday retreat, it would be beneficial. The practice is to go into retreat and find what it is you want to create, the *feeling* of what it is you want to create in your heart, and to sit with it. That is the last part: to sit with it for at least ten minutes. And then to amplify that feeling every time you go back into retreat for this practice once or twice a week.

Know that you are all incredibly powerful creative beings and that your potential is limitless. And we do, indeed, mean limitless.

CHAPTER 6 · MANIFESTATION

When you feel limited, when you feel restricted, when you feel as if you're a victim to your circumstances, come back to this chapter. Allow our words to uplift you, to raise your vibration, and to serve as a reminder of who you are, to remind you there is great power and great strength within you. We wish you could see yourselves as we see you. We see you exactly as you are and nothing less than that. See yourself and all others the same as we do.

And if you are a little unclear as to what it is you want to experience in your life, sit with what it is you *do* know you want to experience. Even if it is a little vague and a little fuzzy, know that it is enough to get the ball rolling, to create space, to create an opening for magic to begin to come into your life. Simply by sitting in whatever it is you know you want, simply by doing *that*, you begin to draw to yourself the life experiences that are a vibrational match for the new high vibration that you cultivated in your sacred retreat. Blessings, dear ones.

CHAPTER 7

The Great Remembering

Hello, friends. It's always a pleasure and a delight to spend time with you in this sacred way, to share our words with you through the channel so that you might feel uplifted and inspired to remember who you are. Indeed, not only is this the great awakening for the human race, but it is also the great remembering. You are remembering who you are. And as this remembering continues, many of you will be surprised to discover you are much vaster than you thought you were.

Many of you who perceived yourself to be mind and body with emotions and a small spiritual component will be quite delighted to discover that you are much more than that.

We can only point to it right now. Little by little, though, you will experience it on your own. And some things are better left to be discovered naturally on your own. This remembering for the human race is not reserved for a few chosen ones. It is not even reserved for those who would label themselves as being spiritual or interested in things of a spiritual nature. It is an awakening that is occurring for *all*. It is a remembering that is occurring for all on some level.

Many of you might say, "Oh, but I know plenty of people who are not remembering at all. They are lost in the darkness." But even those whom you think of as being lost are awakening. Even if it is very subtle, and it is happening beneath the surface and has not been demonstrated in the outside world yet, it is still happening. It is happening for every human being on this planet and for every *living* being on this planet, not just the human race. We speak of the entire animal kingdom and Mother Earth. For she is ascending into the higher realms, taking her rightful place in the universe.

Dear ones, we wish to remind you of the great love we have for you and to remind you of the support you have as you journey onwards through the chapters in this book and through this human incarnation you have been blessed with. This remembering that you are experiencing is also a remembrance of how truly blessed one is to experience a human incarnation. As you probably know, you cannot force gratitude. It must be found in your heart of hearts.

CHAPTER 7 - THE GREAT REMEMBERING

And the best way to find it is to sit and to go on sacred retreat twice a day. And soon, you will discover it is there.

And once you do, then you can bring it out with you into the world and be grateful. For every breath you take is a sacred blessing. For every person that you lay eyes on is a sacred blessing. For every interaction that you have during what you might describe as an ordinary day is a sacred blessing. Invite sacredness into every moment of your life as it unfolds. See every moment as it is, not for anything less.

CHAPTER 8

Be Unproductive

Dear friends, by way of the society you are currently living in, many of you have been taught that you must constantly be going somewhere or doing something that you would label as being productive. We laugh at this because we believe it is fruitful for all of you to engage in activities you might consider *unproductive*, to engage in activities where you are not acting out of the need to accomplish something.

Certainly, there is a time and a place for hard work, work that moves you toward achieving "goals." But that is quite a silly word to us. We say let go of this word goals. The channel is laughing because he has quite a large section about goals in another book of his (*Create Your Dream Life Now, A Workbook & Guide for Manifesting Your Destiny*). So, we are laughing with him. But *he* wrote that book, not us! ☺

So rather than seeking out goals, we encourage you to first go on your sacred retreat to find what it is you are searching for in your heart, whether it's an experience of joy, or an experience of excitement, or an experience of abundance. And rather than using the word goals, we prefer to say:

> ***Seek out events that resonate with what it is you want to experience in your heart center.***

So perhaps, we would trade in the word goals for "experiences of heart resonance." ☺

Dear ones, you do not have to chase after something that exists in what you label as the future. Many of you are like cats trying to catch your own tails. You keep spinning around in circles trying to chase your own tail. But you never catch it because it is impossible to catch. The greatest catch you will ever get is to deeply explore the depths of your own heart and experience the great love that is within you, the great I AM that I AM god-presence that sits within your soul and is available for you to experience in this human incarnation. It is being made available to you now because of what's happening on your planet. Take advantage of *that*, my friends.

> ***This type of opportunity does not come around every incarnation.***

We sound like an advertising campaign, but it is the

CHAPTER 8 - BE UNPRODUCTIVE

truth. This is the commercial that should be on your televisions. This is the post that should be on your social media campaigns. This opportunity to discover what is within yourself does not come around every incarnation. But it is available to you now by the grace of your creator. So, use your time wisely. For every hour that you spend chasing after your tail, if you would devote some time to more *simple* activities that put you into *presence*, rather than racing towards the future, you would have an easier time remembering what is within you.

When you are chasing something that is in front of you, like the cat who tries to catch his tail, you are not present. Your mind is already moving toward the moment you *think* is coming. And in *that* mode, that most people are in most of the time, there is no connection to this god-presence because you are not present.

Here's an example in case some of you are confused. If you're at home in the morning and you have a to-do list, and there are ten things on it, you might set out to check all these things off your list. Now, you're in constant fast forward, moving toward the next thing to do on your list. And in this constant forward motion, you are not present. So, we are going to offer you a very simple way in which you can be present and discover this I AM that I AM god-presence within yourself more easily.

It is imperative in this time of awakening that you spend time doing things that have no future timeline attached to them.

We speak of activities that put you into the sacredness of now. All great spiritual teachers have not only spoken about love as being the highest path, but they have *also* spoken of presence. We do, too. The channel is thinking of gardening, a perfect example of something that puts you into the eternal now and does not have your mind set on a future event. You will know when you are in this state of presence because everything will slow down. Time will actually seem to stop because you will be immersed in a state of deep relaxation and deep contentment with what you are doing.

And it is in these moments of deep relaxation and contentment that the I AM presence within you begins to percolate. So, we encourage you to weave these unproductive activities into your daily routine. They are just as important as going on your sacred retreat twice a day. They are an extension of that. It is going on sacred retreat with your eyes open and your senses engaged. And it is there that you will begin to remember lost parts of yourself.

And just as we said that you won't lose time by going on your sacred retreats, you won't lose time if you spend time doing things your mind considers unproductive. In truth, when you take time for these activities, you are much *more* productive than you would be if you were out and about running to the next place you have to get to. You might *think* of that as productive. But it is not. It is counterpro-

CHAPTER 8 - BE UNPRODUCTIVE

ductive.

Productive, in our eyes, means you are engaging in an activity that helps you to connect to your spirit.

- If you are doing something that helps you connect to the light within you, that is productive.

- If you are doing something that tickles your soul, that is productive.

- If you are doing something that helps you relax, that is productive.

- If you are doing something that helps you experience the love that is in your heart for yourself and all beings everywhere, that is productive.

- If you are doing something to help you to reconnect to the beauty of this planet that you are living on so that you might have reverence for it, that is productive.

And as you devote time to being unproductive, we encourage you to invite others to join with you. That way, they *too* have an opportunity to discover what is inside of themselves. If you call up a friend and say, "I am going to have an unproductive day today," they might say, "I don't believe in having unproductive days. I have a lot to do." Tell them, "There is nothing more important than to engage in an activity that will nurture your spirit and help you to reconnect to what is inside of you."

The next time you go on sacred retreat, at the end of your retreat, before you open your eyes, think of a few things that are unproductive. We are not talking about watching television or looking online for new yoga pants. ☺ We laugh because the channel was doing this yesterday! We are speaking of a moment in time when you stop chasing your tail and you do something that enriches your soul.

We have given permission to the channel to share a list of things that he considers to be unproductive. And when we say that word, we laugh. Because that word, in your society, has such a negative connotation. But in our eyes, we see no "un." We see this list he will make as being much more productive than being in the rat race, in the constant mode of running toward what will come next.

A list of unproductive activities from the channel:

1. Take a hike or nature walk and be fully present with your breath or a mantra as you walk.

2. Admire a tree or any other aspect of nature.

3. Read a book that helps you to still your mind and experience presence.

4. Take a bath with essential oils while focusing on your breath or listening to relaxing music.

5. Garden.

6. Enjoy a cup of tea while being present with your breath.

7. Get a massage and be present with each and every sensation in your body.

8. Immerse yourself in a hobby such as music or painting.

9. Take a day or two to let go of all activities related to your idea of making progress.
10. Spend an entire day in meditation with short meal breaks.

CHAPTER 9

Prayer

Hello, friends. What a pleasure it is to join you in this sacred space of our hearts. For that is where we always meet. And thus, we would ask, before you even begin to read a new chapter, that you sit and close your eyes and enter into your heart space. And take at least ten nice, deep, relaxed breaths into your heart space until you feel as if you're actually there, present in your heart. And only then, open your eyes and begin to receive the words we speak through this channel. And know that we speak them directly into your heart. Your mind receives them, but it is in your heart where they actually vibrate and integrate into your being and into your life.

The channel has a group of Native American guides that have been with him since birth. And the channel recently connected to these Native American guides in a more intimate way. In the same way that we speak through him to you, they also speak through him. We honor their great teachings. Know that any teaching that speaks to your heart and resonates with your inner being is a great teaching. And if the teaching does not speak to you, then it might be a good teaching for somebody else. Today, they would like us, on their behalf, to speak about prayer.

Every teaching that comes through the channel is carefully selected as a teaching that will connect you to your heart and the great love that is within you. Prayer is another practice that can do this. We would like you to pray with your heart. Pray with your heart and pray wholeheartedly. Do not be wishy-washy about your prayers.

Just as we have asked you to commit to the practice of sacred retreat twice a day for fifteen minutes a day for each sitting, if prayer resonates with you, then we would ask you to commit to a daily prayer practice in addition to your practice of sacred retreat. It could be that you pray before your sacred retreat, after your sacred retreat, or as a stand-alone practice.

> *The practice of prayer, my friends, is incredibly simple.*

Place your hands together in front of your heart center and feel a resonance in your heart. Do not begin to pray until you're communicating with your heart. In fact, we would say there is nothing on this planet you should do until you are in tune with your heart. Do not think, do not act, do not speak until you are in your heart center. You will find everything goes more smoothly, and you are more pleased with the results. And then simply, with your hands together in front of your heart center, speak what is on your mind and in your heart. And know that your prayers are heard.

This is what the Native American guides want you to know, that your prayers are, indeed, heard. Even when you think they are not heard, they are. Just because your prayers are not answered immediately does not mean they're not heard. Just because your prayers are not answered as expeditiously as you'd like them to be, doesn't mean they're not being heard. Just because it feels as if you are waiting longer than you should wait doesn't mean your prayers are not heard. Your prayers *are* heard.

The channel is thinking of waiting for a train to arrive, and it seems like it will never arrive, but eventually, it does, and you hop onboard. So yes, prayers are like this. Sometimes, you have to wait a little longer than expected for them to be answered. And sometimes, there might even be delays, and you might have to wait even longer because the universe is setting things up so that it can answer in a way that will please you.

Know that in some way, even if it is not up to your ego's expectations, your prayers will get an answer. And you will know when they're answered. You will have an aha moment when you say, "Oh, this is my prayer being answered. My prayer has been heard, and it has been responded to."

The Native American guides also encourage you to focus on what is most important to you in your prayers and to prioritize two or three things that are of great importance to you in the moment. And continue to pray for those two or three things until your prayers have been answered, until your concerns evaporate.

Faith is imperative in this process, dear ones.

Have faith that your prayers will be answered. We can tell you many stories from ancient times of those who were highly devoted to the creator. And they, too, did not feel as if their prayers were being answered. But they had great faith. So, they kept on praying until their prayers were answered. No prayer goes unanswered. And if you begin to pray for something today, and you fast forward a year, and it hasn't been answered yet in a way that pleases you, you might say to yourself, "The Teachers of the Light were not honest with me." And we would say to you, "Keep praying."

This is one way in which you can activate your creative abilities. Whether you resonate more with the art of manifestation (as we have covered in an earlier chapter, and we will speak of again later) or you resonate with this practice of prayer is up to you.

Perhaps, you will resonate with both. And so, they will both become practices in your life. That is fine. Whatever path you choose is the one that is meant for you. And know that the creator gifted you both of these practices, and we are now simply reminding you they exist. And the creator gave these to you, so you could know you are the creator, too, and that you have just as much power as the creator him-herself. In this quickening that humanity is experiencing, manifestations can happen more expeditiously. And prayers can be answered more expeditiously. So, we remind you that it is a wonderful time to be alive.

Know your power, dear ones. Know you are truly powerful, creative beings. Even if you find yourself in times of trouble or in times of despair, the power is within you to lift yourself up and to know yourself as you truly are. You can experience the god-presence that resides within you. You can experience the great love that resides within you. You can be a beacon of hope and a beacon of light on this planet through everything you do.

You can lead by example.

When you find yourself in troubled waters, when you find yourself in despair as everyone does at one time or another, and you lift yourself up because you know the power to uplift yourself is within you, others can follow in your footsteps. You can reach out your hand and say, "Look, I did it. You can, too. Follow my lead. I will teach you. I will help you."

We offer you many blessings on this sacred day. Please remember that:

- Every day is sacred.
- Every breath is sacred.
- Every step is sacred.
- Every relationship you have is sacred.

We speak even of relationships that just last one or two seconds because you glanced at somebody, and they glanced at you. We speak even of relationships that exist with a few words such as "thank you; have a nice day."

> *Let every word you speak extend from the presence of your heart and the great love that is within you.*

And thus, the creator's vision of heaven on earth shall be fulfilled. And some of you will even be here to see the beginnings of this because it is already happening. The long-prophesized shift is happening now. Can you feel it? If you can't, you will soon. And if you can't, it is likely because your mind is too busy. You are too busy thinking about your life. ☺

Get out of your head. Settle into your heart. See the beauty of all there is. See the shift that is happening before your eyes. And be grateful that you are here at this historic time for humanity. We could go on talking like this forever because we enjoy sharing words of upliftment with you. But the channel has oatmeal that he would like to eat! And he has a yoga class that he has to teach. ☺ We are laughing very loudly. So, we will say, blessings, dear ones. May the greatest love and the greatest light be with you now, forever, and always.

CHAPTER 10

Your Soul Mission

Hello, dear ones. We wish to bring you an important transmission. Some of you are fully aligned with your purpose on this planet. And for that, we congratulate you! Some of you are now just awakening to your purpose on this planet. And for that, we congratulate you, too. Some of you do not know what your purpose is. And as long as you are aware of *that*, we congratulate you, as well. As long as you have the awareness that there is a higher purpose for you, then we congratulate you.

All of you have soul contracts.

These are not the kind of contracts you think of. Meaning if you break it, you are not going to get sued. If you break it, nobody is going to come after you. Nobody will show up at your door and say you have broken your contract; now you must pay. No, this is not the kind of contract we speak of. ☺ Oh, how we laugh sometimes through the channel! We speak of a contract that would better be called a soul mission. For as spirit, before you incarnated into your physical form, you agreed to come here with a purpose, to fulfill a mission. And that is what we call your soul contract.

Many of you, on a soul level, thought it would be fun. And that is part of what inspired you to incarnate into this form at this historic time of awakening. But you came to fulfill a mission, also. Only *you* know how aligned you are with that purpose at this moment in your life. If what you are doing brings you joy because it is an experience you truly enjoy and because you are touching the hearts and souls of other people, then it is quite likely you are aligned with your purpose and that you are fulfilling the mission that you came here to complete.

The mission you came here to complete is not "Mission Impossible." You are not Tom Cruise! You do not have to jump out of helicopters to fulfill it. ☺ The channel cannot believe there was an incarnation in which *he* jumped out of an airplane. He says, "Me? Never." But this disbelief is because there is fear that has not completely left his physical body and his energy field. Much of it has left, but there are still some remnants of it he will continue to let go of.

We have told you that it is likely at times, we might digress. But every time we digress, there is a point we wish

CHAPTER 10 - YOUR SOUL MISSION

to make and something we wish to express that we feel is important. We are planting the seeds for a future chapter.

Know, dear ones, whatever your mission is, it can be fulfilled.

And there are many ways for you to fulfill it. This is part of the beauty of life. There are infinite possibilities for you to express yourself in this world and still fulfill your mission, and thus fulfill your soul contract. And if you do not, it's OK! You will simply pop back into a different body with a slightly modified soul contract based on the new time and new body you are in. And you will go at it again.

So, do you now understand what we mean, dear ones, when we say that all are returning to love and to oneness? Fulfilling your contract is part of this journey. And so, whether you fulfill it now or in a future incarnation is irrelevant. Because you will. It is done. There is no way it cannot be done. But we say why not fulfill it now—when the opportunity is at hand and when your soul brothers and sisters are in desperate need of light workers such as you? We, again, wish to instill this truth upon you:

If you are reading these words, you are a light worker.

You would not be drawn to them if you weren't. There is a certain resonance, a certain vibration that is inherent in these words that only light workers can experience.

Those who are not will read a few pages and put the book down. But the truth is that all are. So, it could be that a few months later, or a few years later, they are drawn to pick up the book again because now they are ready for it. Now they are ready for the teachings we bring.

In regard to fulfilling your soul contract, all we ask of you, dear friends, is that you dedicate the next three sacred retreats to contemplative meditation. At the beginning of your retreat, ask yourself, "Am I fulfilling my soul's mission?" If the answer is yes, then that is wonderful. And if it is, "I don't know," that's fine. Let *that* be your answer. And then revisit the question in the future. And if the answer is no, congratulate yourself for the awareness you have. Celebrate yourself for coming into the awareness that you have a great purpose to fulfill on this planet and that you are opening up to the opportunity to fulfill it.

And then we invite you to ask for guidance from the Teachers of the Light and from any other light beings who resonate with you. Simply say,

"Show me the way to fulfilling my soul contract."

And then you will see, you will begin to receive little bits and pieces of information that lead to clarity. These bits and pieces might come through your dreams, through overhearing conversations, from seeing things that pique your interest, or from what the channel labels as synchronicity, being in the right place at the right time to expe-

CHAPTER 10 - YOUR SOUL MISSION

rience what you need to experience to move you forward along your path in life.

And once you're clear about your mission, it does not mean that you need to leave everything behind and make a drastic life change, although some of you might. It is simply a matter of integration. Integrate whatever your mission is into your life. And in time, allow this soul mission to become the priority in your life. This way, you can touch as many hearts and as many souls as you can while you are here. That is the purpose of a soul contract: to touch as many hearts and souls as you can while you are in this physical form.

It is likely that your soul contract will use the unique gifts you have—that only you have—and that only you can express. You are a unique aspect of the divine. Celebrate that. Celebrate your uniqueness. Celebrate what you, and only you, have to bring to the planet. Rejoice in the gifts you have, and do not keep them to yourself. They were meant to be shared with many. And know that in your uniqueness, you are also one with all your other unique soul brothers and soul sisters. And celebrate your diversity by coming together for your awakening parties.

Indeed, some of you might find yourselves at big parties that celebrate your awakening as a human race. But it is quite satisfactory to have smaller parties, as well. Some of your parties might just have a few people. You might look at the people in the room and think that this person is not like me. Then, you will remember our teachings. Then you will remember that the awakening is here, and it is time to bypass the ego, which is the part of you that's conditioned to think others are different from you.

And with that intention to see others as they are, to see only the god-presence that is within them and not the outward appearance, you will begin to open up to the great love that is inside of you. It is OK if it is a little bit forced at first. But soon, it will become quite natural for you to immediately see the god-presence within someone else, to immediately tune into the sweet quality in your heart, and to feel the love you have for that other person.

And once you have become a master at that, then you will extend it even further. You will extend it to the ones who you consider yourself to be most separate from. For these are the ones who need your love the most. Then, you can extend it to the entire planet. For the entire planet needs your love. Then, you will extend it even further so that the entire galaxy feels it—so that you come into harmony with your galactic friends with the knowing that it is not only the human race that is meant to come into oneness, and it is not only the entire planet that is meant to come into oneness, but it is the entire galaxy and the entire universe.

The channel is just beginning to open up to this now. He is beginning to open up to the awareness that there are other star systems where other light beings like himself reside. And even though these star systems might look very distant in telescopes, they are not very far at all. They are all right here and right now, unfolding into a state of oneness through which connection and heart resonance are available.

So, do you see, my friends, that distance is an illusion? That what you think of as being far away is not so far away? There will be a time when you truly understand these words through your own experience. Right now, we are just planting little seeds that will germinate in the near future.

There is no separation, my friends.

The separation you experience is an illusion. It has been set up that way so you may awaken from the illusion and know that all are one and that love is the thread that ties you all together. This is the beginning of some higher-level teachings that require expanded awareness. We know you're ready for these teachings. Otherwise, we would not transmit them through the channel in this particular book.

- All are returning home.
- All are returning to truth.
- All are returning to oneness.
- All are returning to love.
- All are returning to know that the separation you have felt on this planet is ending.

We remind you to have great love and great compassion for yourself. And we remind you that the courage you seek to share your gifts with the world and to fulfill your purpose is within you. Blessings, dear ones.

CHAPTER 11

Unleash Your Inner Child

Hello, friends. This seems to be a regular occurrence—that we meet you here in the space of the heart! And for that, we take great joy. It is important to us and the channel that you experience the lightness and the humor that is part of our energy signature. Let it remind you not to take life as seriously as most of you do. Remember to lighten up and to allow yourself, every now and then, to be like a child, to return to the innocence and freedom you had before you were conditioned to become an adult. This conditioning began the moment you came out of your mother's womb. As people progress from childhood into adulthood, that conditioning begins to shape them and mold them into what many consider to be mature adults.

We encourage you to let go of your maturity every now and then and to play and to allow that playfulness to bring a greater sense of freedom and joy into your heart. You have many holidays. For some, you are not so concerned about what the holiday means but rather that you get a day off work. ☺ If it were up to us, there would be a holiday "play like a child day" for all. This would be a wonderful holiday to have. So, let go of your responsibilities and play.

"Let go of my responsibilities," you say? "Are you (the Teachers of the Light) crazy? How can I do that?" We are not asking you to let go of them entirely. We are asking you to pause every now and then to enjoy the innocence of your inner child. The inner child is the part of you that lived in complete freedom and in complete joy when you were very young. Some of you might even remember some of these experiences. Others may not. The channel recently became aware of his inner child, and it said, "I want to play."

The more you can become child-like, the more you will connect to your spiritual nature.

And you will find that when you return to your responsibilities, you might relate to them a little bit differently. You might bring some of your inner child back into what you call the real world and experience it with more light-heartedness.

There is not much more that needs to be said about this topic. And based on the energy of today, we do not feel compelled to get into another topic. We would rather come back *after* you have given yourself permission to play like

CHAPTER 11 - UNLEASH YOUR INNER CHILD

a child. Even if it is for a very short amount of time, do it before you journey on to the next chapter. We encourage you to ask yourself, "What can I do that my inner child would enjoy tremendously? What can I do that would bring a smile to my face and joy to my heart?" And then, do it. And we are asking the channel to do the same. For he needs this practice, as well.

Anything you can do to lighten up and unstick yourself from being an adult all the time benefits this journey of the heart. Anything you can do to lighten up and smile more will be beneficial for opening up to the great love within you. The channel is reminded of something he observed yesterday. He was sitting having a snack before his workout, and he noticed a young child who was playing for no other reason but because she wanted to enjoy herself. This is what we ask of you as well.

When the channel himself became aware of his inner child recently, his inner child spoke to him quite clearly, and it said, "I would like to go to the beach and run up and down this beach with a kite in my hand." And the adult part of the channel said, "OK, we'll do it. I will honor you. And we will go and have fun." And yet, quite some time has passed, and he has yet to do it. So, do not delay. We speak to both the channel and to you. Give your inner child the permission to express the freedom and the joy he or she is yearning for. And then bring a little bit of it back into your adult life that is filled with responsibility and obligation.

You will find little ways of doing it that do not impede

your responsibilities but rather add some lightness to them. With great love in our hearts for the entire human race, we say blessings, *children*! Because today, we speak to your inner child. And we say, let it be free! Un-adult yourself for at least fifteen minutes today or tomorrow—preferably, for a longer period of time. Do not worry; your adult self will not go anywhere. It will be waiting for you to return. ☺

The channel makes this joke when he teaches yoga classes sometimes. He says, "Don't worry; your thoughts won't go anywhere. They'll be there for you to pick up after class. But for now, let them go." So, we say, for a short period of time, let your adult self go. You can pick it up after you have fun being a child again. And when you pick it up, you will feel better than you did.

Even the channel is worried about this guidance. He says, "I have to focus. I have to work hard. I have many things to do, including my spiritual practice." And our answer to him as it is to you is all will go better if you give yourself time to express your inner child. You will create space for more flow in your life. You will create space for more openness and receptivity. When you lighten up, what you seek can actually come to you more easily.

Blessings to all. And may you all bless each other, as the child blessed the channel with *her* presence that morning as he received the gift of observing her joy and her freedom. May you also bless somebody today simply by being you, by showing them the love, the compassion, and the kindness that is in your heart. That is all.

CHAPTER 12

Sacred Mornings

Hello, friends! Morning is a sacred time of day. And so, we, the Teachers of the Light, have chosen to transmit the words for this book in the mornings just after the channel rises. For there is a certain level of openness and receptivity that he has at this time of day before he enters the outside world. So, we invite you to make your mornings sacred as well. As we have shared with you, our hope is that in time, you will open up to the sacredness of *every* moment of your day, to the sacredness of every breath you take and every step you take. Let your entire morning be a sacred time to honor the new day.

When you wake up to a new day, the sun, she simply shines in the moment. She does not worry whether she will shine tomorrow. And though she has a memory of her history from the beginning of her creation, she does not concern herself with the rays that she transmitted the day prior.

So, every morning rise like the sun, present to the day that is at hand.

Sit in appreciation of the day. Take your time to get moving. You do not have to jump out of bed and begin running a marathon right away as most of you do. If it is necessary, go to bed much earlier so you can get up on your own without feeling pressured to run somewhere. Give yourself time to sit and relax and enjoy your morning. You will see that by doing this, there is a greater possibility your day will flow with ease.

Create a sacred routine that nourishes you in the morning. And let that sacred routine bless your day. The morning offers you a sacred time to be incredibly present with everything you're doing, whether it's eating a nourishing meal slowly and truly enjoying it as opposed to shoveling it down your mouth, or sipping tea and truly enjoying every sip, or taking some nice deep relaxing breaths with your eyes closed and truly enjoying every breath. Appreciate the life force that is flowing continuously through you, that is gifted to you by the creator who is nourishing and supporting you. We say it is a miracle, friends. And you are part of it. Rejoice in that. Rejoice in the miracle of your morning!

The morning is also a wonderful time to engage in your sacred retreat. If it were up to us, you would rise and go right into your retreat when the mind is quiet from rest.

CHAPTER 12 - SACRED MORNINGS

And then, very slowly, without rushing, open your eyes to the new day and make the rest of your morning sacred. And then bring that sacredness out into your day. Once you discover the sacredness of your mornings, you will have an easier time bringing sacredness into your day and an easier time being present to what the day would like to gift you with.

Stay receptive. Sit back and relax during your day rather than attacking it. You can do all that you need to do but have a different experience of it, a much more relaxed, inviting, receptive experience. Even through those moments you say are not ones you would pick if you didn't have to, you can do this. You can sit back and relax. Even *those* moments will become more easeful, and good things will come out of them.

And the channel thinks it will be good for you to sit in your sacred retreat for longer periods of time occasionally. Don't be afraid to double it every once in a while. That extra time will allow your mind and your body to settle into a deeper state of stillness. And in that deeper state of stillness, your soul will arise, and your heart will begin to shine even more. You will begin to settle even deeper into the great love within you.

If you could imagine for a moment, a sacred wheel of light. At the hub of the wheel is our core teaching. It is the main message we wish to convey to you, which is to open up to the great love and light in your heart center for all beings everywhere. Each practice we give you is like a spoke on this wheel. And all these practices lead to the great love that is in your heart. And that love radiates outward into the world. And with it, you contribute to the creator's vision of heaven becoming manifest on this Earth.

There are many dimensions to reality.

The Earth plane is just one of the dimensions that exist. Other dimensions exist simultaneously in the now. But most are only receptive to and aware of what they see with their naked eyes. Now humanity is beginning to wake up to see there are other dimensions that are all occurring simultaneously in the here and the now. And you are now waking up to the dimension you label as heaven and discovering this dimension can be experienced here and now while you are here in your physical body.

It has been quite some time since this opportunity has presented itself on this planet. Take advantage of it, my friends. Take advantage of the energy of enlightenment that is present and shining even brighter upon you with every day that passes on your Earth timeline.

We are going to refer to the words of the great spiritual teacher John Lennon,

> *"Imagine there's no heaven. It's easy if you try. No hell below us. Above us only sky."*

In his own way, he was referring to the possibility that all dimensions are happening simultaneously here and now and that you can open up to them by connecting to the great love in your heart.

As you do this, it is natural there will be some enlightening. You will lighten up by releasing whatever it is you have picked up in this incarnation and others that is not yours. And anything that is not of love is not yours. We repeat, anything that is not of love is not yours. You have picked it up along the way. You picked it up during your travels and put it in your suitcase. Your suitcase is your mind, your body, and your human energy field. Look within you. See what's yours and what isn't.

And when you discover something that is not yours, as many of you are doing during this awakening, let it go. Call upon us for assistance, and we will help you. Call upon your soul brothers and sisters. Call upon the light workers who are doing healing work on the planet and ask them to extend their hand to you. Ask them to help you lighten your load. Simply say to them, "I want to return to know the love that I am and the love that is within me."

This is the sacred journey you are on, friends. You are here to know the love that you are and to express that love in the world and touch as many hearts and souls with that love as you can. We have spoken of many important things in this chapter. We invite you to perhaps re-read it. Just like when you watch a movie, sometimes you have to watch it twice to make sure you haven't missed anything.

No words can explain the love that is in your hearts, dear ones. But yet, there is a vibration inherent in our words that will create a pathway for you to experience what it is we wish you to experience. And once you are there, once you are truly there, it will feel so delightful you will not feel the need to get up out of your sacred retreat. This is why you see photographs and paintings of great spiritual teachers from many different traditions sitting in meditative poses for very long periods of time. They discovered the great love and the great light that was within them, and they did not feel very inspired to return to the outside world.

They found everything they sought in their lives. They found it within themselves. They looked around them and said, "Well, I do not see it here in the outside world. I see a lot of pleasurable experiences. But I know that even the best of these experiences will come and go like clouds in the sky. So, I will sit until I experience the great love in my heart that is eternal, the great love in my heart that was present before I incarnated as a human being, and the great love that will continue to be in my heart when my soul rises from my body."

This is the great love and the great light we want you to discover. And we want you to find a balance between enjoying the experiences and pleasures of the outside world and coming to know the eternal bliss that you are.

You are eternal bliss.

CHAPTER 12 - SACRED MORNINGS

That is who you are. And once you have a taste of it, please invite others who are ready to get a taste of it to join you. You will see. Once you radiate with this light, those who are ready to experience it will naturally be drawn to you. You can then consider *yourself* a Teacher of the Light, just like us. But we remind you: It is not becoming anybody who you are not already. It is simply remembering what is within you and what you can share with the world.

This might be one of those chapters that you come back to multiple times in your life. You will find there are teachings inherent in this chapter that you align with more as this awakening continues and your own awakening with it.

Many blessings, my friends. We are with you always. You have our unconditional love and support. Let it be enough that *you* know who you are or that you are at least beginning to get a grasp of it. And let it be enough that you have our love and the creator's love.

If others do not see you for who you are because they are closed-minded, because they are not seeing through the creator's eyes, through the eyes of love, let it be OK. Do not be offended. Do not let it take away anything from knowing who you are. Do not let it get to you. Smile and show them great love and compassion rather than contempt, rather than allowing yourself to become a victim. Stay rooted in the truth of your own being.

And if you live with family or with friends, invite them to be part of your sacred morning. It will help you connect. It will serve to bring you together in the name of love. For those of you who have children, they would greatly benefit from your inviting sacredness into your morning and sharing it with them.

CHAPTER 13

A Day of Reception

Hello, friends. It is with great love that we greet you. Today there is nothing to learn and nothing to practice. Today is a day for simply allowing yourself to receive the great love that all of creation has for you. This love flows like a gentle stream from many different aspects of the creator, and we, the Teachers of the Light, are one of those aspects. For those, including ourselves, who know this great love and experience it continuously, we are present in your lives for one purpose and for one purpose only. It is so you might know this great love, too.

So today, dear friends, be open to receiving. If today is not the right day for you to do that, then choose a different day without much delay. Let it be within the next seven days. Call it your day of reception. And on that day, sit for a longer period of time in sacred retreat first thing upon rising. Have a light breakfast. And then go outside somewhere that enables you to connect to nature. The god-presence that you seek is present in all living things, and you can especially feel it through your planet's beauty.

Before you step outside on this day of reception, we ask you to leave all your troubles behind. You can pick them up again if you so desire *after* your day of reception. ☺ But really, commit to leaving your troubles behind for a day. After you spend some time absorbing the peace and the wisdom that is inherent in Mother Nature, allow your intuition to guide you toward any experiences that will nurture your spirit. Most importantly, we want you to relax and unwind.

No matter where you are and what you are doing during this day of reception, stay relaxed. It is only by staying relaxed and open that you can receive. Simply allow yourself to be open to the great love that the creator, who we are part of, has for you. Notice any filters that prevent you from experiencing this great love.

We tell you that once you are completely unfiltered, you will feel the totality of this love. And it will wash over you and bring you great peace and great joy. If you notice that there are filters preventing you from experiencing the depths of this love that we speak of, repeat these words to yourself:

> *"I allow myself to be receptive to the greatest amount of love I can feel from the creator, and*

every aspect of the creator, in this moment of reception. And so it is that I am blessed."

Then as you return to your normal everyday activities, stay receptive. Stay in this state of reception. Be the receiver of the love that is present for you.

We began by saying that there will be no practice for today. And we still honor the words that we have spoken. This experience is not a practice. Because all we are asking you to do is to sit back, relax, receive, and know that without needing to be anybody, without needing to go anywhere in particular, without needing to do anything at all, without needing to accomplish anything, you are complete and whole just as you are. You are loved. And you are that great love as well. And you *are* the presence of perfection simply by being.

CHAPTER 14

Recalibrating the Heart

Dear friends, as you anchor in the new vibration of love that is becoming more present on the planet, we encourage you to make it a priority to check in with yourself. And to ask yourself, "Am I in it, or am I not in it?" You will know. And if you are not in it, get in it! ☺ Close your eyes wherever you are. Take some deep breaths. Put a little smile on your face. Put your attention on your heart center and let it expand, let it open, let it vibrate. And then, and only then, return to what it is you are doing in the outside world.

As you begin to experience deeper sacred retreats and spend longer periods of time in them every once in a while, you will discover that you are rising higher, your body is becoming lighter, and your heart is becoming as wide and open as the sky. It is becoming limitless. And that experience you have in your sacred retreat is now a reference point you can return to at will. And it might not be that you can return to the *highest* reference point you experienced in your sacred retreat, but you can at least recognize when you are far away from it, and you can move back toward it.

> *Let it be your priority to tend, much as a gardener would tend to a garden, to your own heart.*

If you notice that it is not as vibrant as it should be, do some watering. Tending to your own heart should be even easier than it is to tend to a garden. You don't have to go outside and get your hands dirty. ☺ You simply have to close your eyes and come back into it, to open as wide as you can in the moment. You will begin to become more aware of the moments you are in your heart center and the moments you are not. For the moments you are, there will be at least some joy simply because you are present in your heart. This joy we speak of is not dependent on experiences in the outside world. It is simply dependent upon your presence, your willingness, and your intention to be present in your heart.

We have said a lot about the word present because it is an important one. The channel often thinks the present moment is called the present because it is indeed a present, and we agree. And it becomes an even *more* beautiful present if you are in your heart center.

CHAPTER 14 - RECALIBRATING THE HEART

The present moment sparkles when you are in your heart. It sparkles with the quality of joy.

And so, not only are you weaving in and out of your sacred retreats, but you are also weaving in and out of the depths of your heart. It is not expected that your heart will be wide open like the sky all the time. But we intend to invite you to start experiencing your heart in this manner more often than not.

Dear friends, this is our teaching for today. It is a short chapter, but it is all that is needed. For once we feel we have shared our perspective, once we feel we have said enough to have lifted your vibration, to have taught you the lesson we want you to experience, we will end the transmission.

CHAPTER 15

Sitting in Appreciation

Dear friends, it is quite likely this will be one of the shortest chapters in the book because not much needs to be said. So, we are going to get straight to the point. It is *imperative*, and yes, we know that is a strong word, that you sit and simply be grateful for the present moment without any agenda at all, without feeling any need to do anything at all. If you cannot do that for at least a few minutes a day, then you are missing the mark. Then, you will wake up one day, and you'll realize you were always trying to get somewhere, but you were never truly here. Does that make sense to you?

It is as simple as sitting and appreciating your breath. That's it. It is as simple as appreciating that you exist as part of creation. That is a priceless moment, friends, to sit in gratitude, without feeling the pull to go somewhere, to do something, or to work toward accomplishing something.

So, we ask you, friends, in addition to your practice of sacred retreat, take a few minutes to do *this* every day. It could be part of your sacred retreat practice. But in some way, it must be there as part of your life, every day. And we actually encourage you to do it in *addition* to your sacred retreat practice. Because even during your sacred retreat practice, you might find there are days when you are sitting and subtly intending to accomplish something. Maybe you want to still your mind, or open your heart, or raise your vibration, or experience more love and joy, or relax. Or all of that. But even if it is subtle, there is still something you're moving toward, yes?

What we are asking you to do is to move toward nothing at all and to be incredibly appreciative of your breath and that you are part of creation, that you are part of this *miracle*. It is indeed a miracle, friends. And it is only by taking this time to sit in appreciation that you can tune in to that miracle. Just being part of creation is a miracle. Just breathing is a miracle.

And then, when you open your eyes and engage with the outside world, you will be more grateful. While gratitude cannot be forced, it is very easy to sit in appreciation. And by doing *that*, you will feel more grateful for what is around you. You will feel more grateful for what you might label as the ordinary moments of life. And as the channel begins his day and makes his oatmeal, he will be more grateful than he would have been if he had not taken a few

CHAPTER 15 - SITTING IN APPRECIATION

minutes to be appreciative in this way.

Sitting in appreciation, this is the practice, friends. Sitting in appreciation of the miracle you are part of. Blessings.

CHAPTER 16

Love Heals All Wounds

Do the work, friends. Heal what needs to be healed. Love what needs to be loved. We are speaking of the traumas you have gone through, either in this incarnation or in others that you carried into this one. Many of you aren't even aware of these traumas because you are too busy living your lives.

Go within. See what is there. Allow yourself to feel the trauma at the moment of its original experience. Let it go. Allow your heart to crack open. Allow the tears to flow through you. And then love the wounded part of you. You might ask, "How do you do that?" Well, there is a source within you that is love and nothing but love. Connect to *this*. And from this space of infinite, unconditional divine love, shine light upon that wounded part of you so that it may heal. This is the work that much of humanity, in one way or another, is undergoing now.

You are going through it for one reason and one reason only, to return to knowing yourself as you are. Complete, whole, one with that which you can never be apart from. We say this to you, those who are reading this book and the channel himself. You are almost home. So, keep going. Keep doing the work you are doing. And if you are not doing it *yet*, but you know you need to, then begin doing it. Now is the time. Now is the time for healing the planet, releasing all traumas, and loving all wounds. Love heals all wounds. This is the truth.

Today, the channel was taking a walk near the beach. And a young child passed him on her scooter. And she was having the best time that anybody could possibly have. She was experiencing so much joy and so much freedom that she could not contain herself. In fact, without caring about who was listening, she joyfully yelled, "giddyup, giddyup, giddyup!" *This* is who you are becoming. And the work we encourage you to do is the work that is necessary for you to return to this original state of pure freedom, pure love, and pure joy without the programming and conditioning you acquired as you became adults.

We tell you, friends, whether you believe it or not right now, this joy you seek, this freedom you seek, this love you seek is within you. So, keep doing the work that is necessary until you experience yourselves as you truly are—until you experience your true nature as this little girl did so beautifully. It was no accident the channel passed her by. It

CHAPTER 16 - LOVE HEALS ALL WOUNDS

reflected what is in his spirit. And this is what the universe wanted to show him. And this is what we want to show you, as well.

Perhaps you can see her in your mind's eye—flying by like the wind, uncontained. Her joy, her freedom, her pure expression of the godliness within her was uncontained. This is what we want for all of you. We want the freedom, and the joy, and the godliness that is within you to be uncontained, to be liberated. And the best way to do this is to go within to discover it is all within you. And then, to give yourself permission to express it through the beautiful being that is you.

Let there be no holding back. Now is *not* the time to hold back. Now is the time to express the beauty that is you. Now is the time to express the godliness within you. Now is the time to express the love within you. Now is the time to express the unbridled, uncontained, unfiltered joy that is within you and is you.

This is the work we speak of, friends. At times, it might feel a little bit arduous. But we tell you it is well worth it, to be liberated, to be free. What a feeling that will be for everybody on this planet—to be liberated from all your programming, from all your conditioning, from all your fears, from all of it. And to experience yourself as you truly are and to know that all are the same. To know that the same god-presence that is within you, that is bubbling up inside of you as love and joy, is within all.

This is the path, friends. So, keep going. Keep going

until you are you again. You're getting there. Even in the moments when your mind, your ego, tricks you into thinking you are not getting anywhere, you are one step closer to home. You are one step closer to union with the source of your being-ness. You are one step closer to realizing there was never any "there" to get to because it was all there already. Celebrate *that,* friends. Celebrate what is inside of you.

With great love, we wish you many blessings on this path you are on. Continue to be courageous. It takes some courage, does it not, to move beyond what it is you've known in the past—to move beyond fear—to move beyond programming—to move beyond conditioning—to move beyond the person you thought you were. Yes, it takes courage to do all that. But it is well worth the courage to return home, to know all of yourself, and to *express* all of yourself during this great awakening.

The children are your teachers.

When you see a child fully expressed in a freedom, in a love, in a joy that reflects who you are, you might say, "Oh, but I am not that. I am an adult. I have responsibilities." We say no. What you see in that child, *that* is you. That is the *real* you. That is who you *really* are.

We will leave you with this, friends. If you are to make a list of your goals, put as number one to feel the freedom, the pure expression of love, and the fulfillment of

CHAPTER 16 - LOVE HEALS ALL WOUNDS

joy already contained within you. What more could you ask for than that, right? When you seek out experiences in the outside world, we say *that* is what you are *really* seeking regardless of what the mind is seeking. And so perhaps it is time to do some rearranging of your priorities.

The channel says, "Oh, but what about people with responsibilities?" We say to move in the right direction, and you know what that direction is, yes? And if you're completely bewildered, ask for guidance, and you will receive it. You may pray for it if you like, or in any other way that you resonate with, to ask for guidance, guidance to once again experience your godliness as that child did without reservation.

We remind the channel and remind you, too, to seek *this* out through all you do. We guarantee there is at least one thing you can do today or tomorrow to move in that direction, even if you have to give yourself a little nudge, even if you have to make yourself feel a little uncomfortable, even if you have to do the work we've spoken of in this chapter. There is a way, friends. There is a way forward toward experiencing what is within you.

It is only because the channel is experiencing at least some of this freedom and the joy and the love that is within him that we can speak of it. We can speak of nothing the channel has not experienced. This is actually an agreement his spirit made with the energies that speak through him. For he does not have any desire to bring guidance and support for humanity that is above and beyond his understanding, which only comes by way of direct experience.

The channel does not mind our saying he is still a little locked up. Many of you feel the same way. It is time to unlock yourselves. And so, we will leave you with this. We hope if you see the channel one day—that he *himself* is riding on a scooter laughing and smiling, full of joy, yelling "giddyup, giddyup, giddyup." And if you see him, and he is not, and he looks serious, then tell him, "Be like the child you saw on that day in sunny California. Be like the child." And we hope he looks back at you and says, "Let us be children together. Let us frolic in that way."

Now is the time to unlock yourselves.

We hope this gives you permission, the permission you're all seeking, to be yourselves. You do not need anybody's permission to be yourself. But yet, we give it to you so that you feel our support and our encouragement. And know that we are smiling upon you every time you choose to unleash, to set free, and to liberate what is within you in the name of freedom, in the name of love, and in the name of joy. And when you do *that*, others will be touched too. And they will give themselves permission to take the ride with you.

They will no longer feel ashamed, or embarrassed, or afraid, or any of those things that arise from past experiences. And once you all give yourselves permission to be free, you will have so much fun doing it that you will con-

CHAPTER 16 - LOVE HEALS ALL WOUNDS

tinue to do it repeatedly until it becomes your natural way of being on the planet.

What a delightful time we have had with you. It has been quite some time since the channel has made himself available for the energies to flow through him in this way. We say it has been for multiple reasons. In his mind, he thought to himself, "Well, the book is almost complete." And it is also because he has been focused on other projects, most of them which are quite meaningful and purposeful.

Now we ask him, and we ask you, to create an affirmation for yourselves that embodies the teaching of this chapter and to put it somewhere where you can read it so that you don't forget about it. We don't want you to feel inspired at this particular moment, but then to wake up tomorrow and leave it behind you. Continue to remind yourselves of it. And every day, do something that embodies the teaching.

If there is healing that needs to be done, then do *that*. And if there is love and joy and freedom within you that you need to express, then do *that*. Or perhaps you will find yourself doing both at the same time or at least on the same day. We feel as if we are complete. We hope you feel this teaching is complete, also. It is an important one. It puts things in perspective, does it not? What you *thought* was important perhaps is not as important as you thought.

CHAPTER 17

Let Go and Flow

The channel knows when the words are ready to flow through him by the way he is feeling vibrationally. And it is quite humorous to *us* how on occasion, he will sit intending to channel instantaneously as if he can turn on a switch and the energy will begin to flow. It is his ego that thinks he can do *that* just because he has seen other channels do it. Yet, he is learning how to channel in his own way. And the greatest teacher he will ever have is himself.

You might see another channel who can channel immediately. But perhaps, the energy is not as high as another's energy. And *that* is why he sits. He sits to raise *his* vibration so it can *match* the vibration of the energy he wants to come through him. Upon hearing the word *match*, the channel's mind turns to romance. ☺ But we don't want to speak much about it. We said it is of great importance to focus on your *own* personal vibration. And *then* what you seek, without much effort, will appear in front of you.

It is like this with channeling *and* with finding a romantic match. Perhaps there will come a day when the channel's vibration will be more consistent. And then, with the snap of a finger, he will channel. But for now, he needs to sit. He needs to meditate so that his vibration rises to meet ours. When you begin to have new, delightful experiences in your life, they are, in part, because you have done the work to prepare for them. But even more so, it will be because you will have raised your vibration to match those experiences so that, voila, they may appear in your own life.

We are speaking, of course, of the synchronistic meetings you have with the people whom you are meant to meet—the types of meetings that can change your life in very dramatic ways. It does not happen haphazardly. Nor does it happen solely because you are working hard. That's just a little piece of it. It also happens because you are working to raise your vibration.

And so it is, somebody might try to label you. They might meet you, and they might say, "What do you do?" And they might expect you to say that you are a lawyer or a doctor or a this or a that. Perhaps you will shake them up by saying, "I am an individual expression of the divine who is raising his or her vibration. *That* is who I am." And they might say, "What?" That makes us laugh. Most likely because of the new energies, they will actually be quite interested in what you have to say. They will find it a lot more interesting than if you had identified yourself in the way that people normally do. And that will give you an opportunity, by way of your high vibration, to raise *their* vibration. Isn't that delightful?

So, it is all right to let go of the way society has acclimated you to labeling yourselves. As you know by now, we like to give you practices you can incorporate into your everyday life. That is a good one for you. Begin to identify yourself in a new way. Begin to identify yourself as an energetic being rather than a "this" or a "that," rather than a man or a woman, rather than somebody with this sexual preference or *that* sexual preference, rather than somebody who voted for *him* or voted for *her*, rather than somebody who likes *this* kind of food but doesn't like *that* kind of food.

> *Begin to identify yourself in a more truthful way that gets down to the heart of the matter.*

You are an energetic being that is having quite an interesting experience in physical form. And as you are navigating this experience, your focus is raising your vibration and maintaining it. The channel has had some difficulty doing *that* lately. He sits, he raises it. Then he steps out into the world and well....You know what happens because it happens to you, also. It is the nature of being here on this planet.

For some of you, the channel included, raising your

vibration needs to be something you do quite frequently during the day, not just in meditation. If the channel did that earlier, he would not have been so grumpy prior to this channeling. And perhaps, he would not have had to sit for such an extended period of time to raise *his* vibration so the words could begin to flow through him.

It is quite interesting to us. There is still a little bit of the personality of the channel who drops in every now and then and says, "I would like to talk about *this*." And *we* find it quite amusing. And we say, "No, that is not the purpose of these transmissions." The channel is continuing to get out of the way so that *we*, the higher frequencies, can come through and so that the higher frequencies of life can begin to frolic with him in this time-space reality he is part of. Like many of you, he is standing on the *cusp* of it. Meaning the great change that you are all seeking is much closer than any of you think.

We encourage *you*, as we do the channel, to let go of control and to allow yourself to take the next steps. As it is with the channel, you might have your fears. And to you, they might seem very real, as they do to the channel. For there are a lot of "buts" that his personality says, "Oh, but!" Let go of *those*, friends. There must be a time for letting go of whatever it is that holds you back, such as a lack of belief in yourself—or a but—the but that is the doubt of the ego.

During this great time of awakening, a time in which your participation and your light are very much needed, we urge you to let go and to step fully forward on the path you know you are meant to travel on.

There are very few of you reading these words who do not know what that path is, even though it might not be *completely* clear to you. In other words, you might not know exactly what trees you will pass along the way. You might not know exactly what birds or animals you will encounter. As the analogy points out, you don't know exactly what to expect. Perhaps, things are a little bit fuzzy; yet you know. You have a sense of knowing the path you should be on in your life. And we say simply let go and flow. In fact, those words will be the title of this chapter.

And *please*, allow yourself to have some fun as you go. Stop taking life so seriously! It is not meant to be that way. And if your ego chimes in and says "but," give yourself permission to let that go and to return to the innocent joy of knowing that you are taken care of in the present moment by a creator that loves you very much and by a planet that has great, great, great love for you. Take delight in that as we have been asking the channel to do.

Appreciation, joyful appreciation is always the essential practice.

And in joyful appreciation, you can let go and flow. It often comes to pass that by the end of these transmissions, the channel is feeling blissful. From *his* perspective, the transmission could continue indefinitely, perhaps all night until the break of dawn. Yet, when it is complete, from the higher perspective, then it is complete.

The channel is now thinking of something, and it's quite relevant. So, we'll add it here. Never compare yourself to anybody else and say, I should be doing it *that* way. Allow yourself to find your *own* way. You might see somebody else is doing something that resonates with you. And it might lead you in a particular direction. But *never* try to emulate what anybody else is doing. In the old energy, in the old paradigm, perhaps you could emulate someone else. Not anymore.

As you move into this *new* energy, into this *new* paradigm, you are free to create something uniquely you, something that is your unique personal frequency, that is yours and yours only. So, let others do what they're doing. And do what *you* are meant to do. The channel had many experiences lately when he was tempted to compare himself to someone else and say, "Oh, I should be doing *that*. I should be doing it the way *he* is doing it."

No, you should simply follow your own impulses and create something quite magical that nobody has done before and that nobody could ever do again. And if you meditate often, then the inspiration will come so that you don't even need to consider following in anyone else's footprints. But rather, you will be free to create your own path. That is it for today, friends.

CHAPTER 18

Receiving Divine Guidance

Hello, friends. At this moment, the channel is doing his best to get out of his own way, as we always instruct him to do, so the transmission can come through.

Dear ones, you all have your own transmissions that would like to come through.

Often, we tell the channel to *pause* his daily routine to create space for his own personal transmissions to come through. This is what he labels as his intuition. For if he is too busy in the doing, then he can't receive the guidance that wants to come through. Recently, he has been working diligently on purposeful, meaningful activities in his life. In fact, he had a little motto, "Keep working hard." And, in a way, it worked. But both you and the channel know when that motto is *truly* serving you and when it is not. You know when it is taking *away* from what is truly important in your lives.

What's truly important is to have a sense of balance, find inner peace, give yourself time to play like a child, and do whatever else is *truly* meaningful for you. And so it is, friends, if it happens to be that you are working hard to accomplish what you are meant to accomplish as part of your soul mission, then that is good. But it is also good to take the pauses, to take the moments of rest, to become *receptive* to the *stream* of divine guidance that wants to come through you.

When the divine guidance comes, it might point you in a different direction, one where your hard work becomes even *more* meaningful. The divine guidance can lead you in a new way, in a new direction. It could be as simple as one sentence or a few sentences of divine guidance that comes through. It could be by way of a clairaudient or clairvoyant message. It could just be a sense of knowing. It could be the synchronicity of being in the right place, at the right time, to *receive* the guidance. But it is necessary, every now and then, to take that pause from your hard work so that you may receive it.

From our perspective and from the channel's perspective and life experience, it is most often in the pauses that you can truly receive divine guidance. You might think of the pause as a space in which the divine guidance has the opportunity to enter. The channel recently referred to it as

CHAPTER 18 - RECEIVING DIVINE GUIDANCE

a day of sabbath, meaning a day of rest. He simply stops, takes a break from his normal routine, and allows the guidance to come in.

It does not necessarily mean that you must spend the entire day in sacred retreat or that you must go on a vision quest. But it is imperative that you pause in a way that is appropriate for *you*. For example, yesterday, the channel's pause was to do some reading instead of what he might label as the more meaningful, purposeful work. He allowed himself to take a walk to his favorite coffee shop to get his favorite chocolate croissant and do some reading. Then, he returned home to relax and read some more. And it is in *this* space that he received an important message that is meant to guide him forward in an even more purposeful direction than he is already on.

So, take the pauses, friends. Take them at least once a week or whenever it is you know it is really necessary for you to take the pause. The channel knew because he was already receptive enough to hear the divine guidance that said, "It is time to take a day of rest—to take a pause, to create space." So, he did.

If you are not receptive enough to hear *that*, then perhaps you simply need to make it part of your routine—a routine pause, a routine rest—so you may receive what it is you are meant to receive. And then, when you jump back into the daily grind, you will have the added insight that makes your daily routine more meaningful. Because there will be something new added to it by way of the divine guidance you received. We are laughing because that is actually the name of the coffee shop where the channel got his croissant yesterday (The Daily Grind).

When you take that pause, you are actually creating space to grow. And this is what many of you want, is it not? To continue growing? And for as long as you are present, in the form you are in, you are meant to continue growing. It is the nature of the human being to always seek this out, to have a desire to be growing. And so, the divine guidance that will come through will very likely be divine guidance presented to you so you can continue to grow.

We will be even more specific and use the recent example from the channel's life. During his pause, he was told it is time to hire somebody to assist him with planning events so his work can touch the hearts and souls of more people. It is time for more people to gather around him. And he heard that message. But he would not have heard it if he had not listened to the impulse to pause and rest. But he did. He listened. And he received. Now, he will continue to do what he was doing prior to his rest, but he will do it with this new knowledge that will help him to grow and expand.

In one way or another, this is the path you are all on, friends. You are all on the path of expansion. Can you feel *that*? We believe you can. If you are reading these words, then you are in a state of expansion. We feel you have received our message. And we and the channel want you to know that this pause, or whatever else it is you would like

CHAPTER 18 - RECEIVING DIVINE GUIDANCE

to label it, does not come in place of, in exchange for, your daily sacred retreat practice. It is in addition to it.

One of the benefits of your daily sacred retreat practice is that you will become more receptive to divine guidance.

And you will begin to receive it more often because your mind will be still. Your heart will be open. You will be more relaxed. And because of all those things, you can receive divine guidance more often. You can begin to receive it every day if you please. And wouldn't it be delightful to be guided by your higher self and by those who love you (we are speaking of your guides and your angels) on a regular basis? This will happen through a committed sacred retreat practice.

And then, when you take the pause, the day of rest, or the sabbath, or whatever it is you like to call it, even *more* divine guidance can come through to you. And you can continue to step forward on your path in new and exciting ways that please your mind and your spirit.

And we want to say one more thing, which we are telling the channel directly as well. We want you *all* to give yourselves permission to play more. We have transmitted entire teachings about this, but it is too easily forgotten, especially if your motto is "keep working hard." Please give yourselves permission to play, to have fun, to unleash your inner child. Even if it is just for a few hours every week, truly allowing yourself to play. That, too, is a very necessary pause in any work you're doing.

And you do not have to do it alone. You'd be surprised to find there are others who would like to join you and have fun with you, especially those who you think would *never* want to do it with you. These are the ones who need it the most! These are the ones who just might be the most receptive to your invitation to come and have some fun with you. That is it for today, friends. Blessings.

CHAPTER 19

Tuning the Heart

Hello, friends. There are things that you do in your life with regularity. In your vocabulary, you use the word habit to describe this. And though some of you might have habits that you wish to kick ☺, it is our preference today to speak of your *good* habits and to invite you to add one more good habit into your routine. It is the habit of closing your eyes, going within, and retuning yourself to your heart center. Yes, it is true; we have spoken of this quite recently. And yet, we speak of it again, meaning it is obviously of great importance.

The channel is a musician. When he picks up his guitar, he knows immediately whether the strings are in tune or not. And even if a string is just somewhat out of tune, he can easily tell there is something amiss; there is something that needs adjusting. And he tunes the string back to its

proper tuning.
- The tuning your heart should be in is *love*.
- The tuning your heart should be in is *expansiveness*.
- The tuning your heart should be in is *radiance*. For it is meant to be shining bright!
- The tuning your heart should be in is *without limitation*, beyond the mind's preferences.

And so, we ask you to sit as often as needed and to listen to the tune your heart is singing. And if you are in tune with all that we have just spoken of, that's fantastic. Then, you can open your eyes and continue your day from that heart-space. But if there is something amiss, we ask you to sit and tune your heart to the right note.

Just as the low E string on a guitar is meant to be playing the low E, your heart is meant to be playing the note of love. So, sit as long as you need to sit, as often as you need to, to tune your heart to this great love. And if there is a day when you say to yourself, "My heart will not tune. I cannot even feel it," that's all right. Then, at the very least, sit and still your mind. This way, you are at least inviting yourself into a space in which tuning becomes possible.

And if you sit with this intention of tuning your heart every day, as often as needed, you will find that little by little, with your intention only, by placing your awareness in your heart center, you begin to tune into the great love within you. This exercise is like a mini sacred retreat. Take as many as you need to; spend as much time as possible tuned to the great love within you. This is something the channel is working on himself.

If you need something outside of yourself that will help you tune your heart, that is fine as long as it does not become a crutch you go to every time you need to tune. If you are using something outside of yourself to tune your heart, it's like riding a bicycle with training wheels. It is all right for a short period of time while you learn, but then you need to take off the training wheels and go at it on your own.

So, if you need, you might look at the beauty of a flower and feel the love in your heart for the flower. It might seem silly, but it works. If you have a pet, you might sit and feel the love you have for that pet. If you have a friend, or a partner, or a family member whom you have great love for, you can simply sit with that love.

These are ways in which you can tune the heart using something outside yourself. But we remind you, the best way of tuning is to sit and close your eyes and do it independently. For ultimately, you do not need anything that is outside yourself to tune into the great love and the great light that is within you. All that is needed is you.

And so, we refer to the wise words of one of the *many* teachers who has been present on your planet. He said, "The kingdom of heaven lies within." He didn't say you need to go and look everywhere to find it. Every great teacher said this in one way or another. So, look within, my friends. Look within for what it is you are seeking.

There is no other teaching needed for today. And some of you might say, "Oh, but I have heard this teaching already. I am ready for a new one. Bring it on!" ☺ But there is no other teaching greater than this one. And this is why it is being repeated in a different way. Because every teaching must come back to the place where it originates, the heart center. And it is imperative at this time of awakening that you find your way back there, somehow, some way.

And to be quite frank, after you read this book, if all that you gain is an ability to close your eyes, to be with the sweetness of your breath, and to touch your heart in a way you never have before, then we accomplished our mission. For that in itself is the teaching. Everything else is like icing on the cake. And so, before you run off to whatever it is you are doing today, or before you flip the page to the next chapter, we ask you to close your eyes, to be with your breath, and to tune into the great love within you.

And we remind you to do these practices one at a time. And so again, we invite you to read only one chapter at a time. And to perhaps, even take a few days or even a week or two before you read the next one. Until you can honestly say to yourself, "I am now embodying the teaching of this particular chapter. I am now vibrating with this new vibration that the Teachers of the Light have shared with me."

Then, move on to the next. And you will keep climbing higher until your feet are still touching the Earth, but you feel as if you are so tall that your heart and your awareness are centered in the dimension that we speak to you from.

CHAPTER 19 - TUNING THE HEART

We will end by saying this:

Once your heart is tuned to the note it is destined to be tuned to, your entire experience of life will change.

And we remind you that no matter how busy you might be, this is an invitation that all who read these words may receive and experience. We see the possibility is present for every one of you to tune your heart so that you may experience this great love and great light. Blessings!

CHAPTER 20

Finding the One

Dear ones, we wish to speak exclusively to those who are seeking a romantic partner in life or those who have a romantic partner but already know he or she is not the right fit. If you are to embark on this practice of tuning the heart on a regular basis, you will find you will align with the very person you're seeking.

We refer to the chapter entitled "Manifestation," where we spoke of going in before going out. It's like this with finding the right partner. Although, it is not finding anybody. It is simply coming into resonance with the great love you discovered within yourself. Then, it's only natural that someone else who has also awakened to the great love within themselves shows up in your life. The person you're seeking will magically show up on your doorstep.

You might think to yourself, "It is a miracle," but it isn't.

It is just the way the universe works. Once you are tuned to the vibration of love, it will show up. And so, if that particular person is not in your life yet, or you seem to be attracting the wrong kind, it is because you need to do more tuning. And once you are in a relationship, *continue* to tune on a regular basis.

And we encourage your partner to read this and to do his or her own tuning. For when you are in a relationship, it is necessary that both parties take responsibility for keeping their hearts in tune. If you keep your heart in tune to the great love within you, you will help your partner do the same. And if they, too, keep their heart in tune to the great love within them, then your partnership will be quite blissful. And when you are out of tune with each other (even in the best relationships, there is a little bit of disharmony sometimes), then you can come back into a state of harmony quickly because you both know about tuning.

Many people like to complain, "Oh, I haven't met the right one yet. When will I meet him? When will I meet her?" Or they say, "I have met this person, and they do not fit the bill. Why do I keep meeting the wrong people?" We say meet yourself first. Meet the great love within *your* heart first. And once you have done *that*, trust that the right one will show up at the right time.

CHAPTER 21

The End of Separation

Blessings, friends. There are some of you, and you know who you are, who went on one or two sacred retreats, continued reading the book, and have yet to return to the practice of sacred retreat. ☺ We shared it with you very early because it is the foundation upon which you must build the journey into your heart center. If you are one of those, and please know that we smile and send you great love and sit in joy as we speak these words to you, we give you a little gentle push to really give it a go for the forty days we suggested.

At first, you might feel restless in your sacred retreats. At first, you might have thoughts such as "This is not working! Maybe it works for *other* people, but it does not work for me." Or perhaps you say, "This is a waste of my time." These are natural experiences to have when you begin this practice. But stick with it. It is only by committing to it that you will open up to the great love within you. And it is only by experiencing this great love that our other teachings will resonate more with you.

Often the channel wishes for us to speak through him right away, and we say not yet. We are teaching him how to sit deeper and deeper into the presence of *his* own heart before the words come through him. We share this with you, friends, to remind you there is nothing of greater importance than sitting and opening to the great love and the great joy in your heart. It is only *then* that you should begin to open yourself up to expressing yourself. It is only *then* that you should open up to be a channel for the expression of the god-presence that is flowing through you and all around you.

This is the practice:

- Sit. Get into love.
- Open your eyes.
- Participate in the world.
- Repeat. ☺

Become the turtle. Become the one who weaves into and out of the world. Now that the channel has been sitting for about ten minutes and allowing our words to come through him very slowly, he is feeling an expansiveness in his heart center he didn't feel when he sat and closed his eyes initially.

Dear ones, if it takes you one hundred sittings to get a

CHAPTER 21 - THE END OF SEPARATION

taste of it, that is perfectly fine. We say, accept the journey you are on. Embrace it. Commit to it, and you will be victorious. And the victory we speak of is not winning a race, or achieving a goal, or winning a competition, or even being well known for what it is you do. The victory, friends, is to know yourself as you are, to experience your true self, not everything else outside of it.

Every time the channel comes back to sit in his heart, he says to himself, "Ah, this is it. *Now*, I am back home." And this is why they say home is where the heart is. No matter where you are, no matter what it is you are doing, you should always be home. We want to see for you the same as we want to see for the channel. We want him to be home all the time, not just sometimes. It does require practice. And it certainly requires what he calls consciousness, to be conscious of when you're at home and when you're not.

Sacred retreat is what will help you to *cultivate* this consciousness. You are actually cultivating many wonderful qualities in sacred retreat. You are cultivating a heightened state of awareness. You are cultivating a heightened state of receptivity. You are cultivating a heightened state of focus. You are cultivating deep relaxation and giving your body a chance to heal. You are cultivating a new perspective that will change the relationship you have with everything in your life. And you are tuning back into the great love that is in your heart.

Now, do you see why it is such an important practice? And if you are not doing it yet, you might return to the beginning of the book and start again. We are laughing through the channel; we don't expect you to do that. But we do want you to understand this is the way into your heart, and it is the way out to a much more enjoyable experience of life.

And this you will see in time. As the channel is seeing now through his own eyes, as a result of his sacred retreat practice, his experience of life has changed. He is much steadier. That is to say, there are fewer ups and downs. He is much more focused. He feels a little lighter. He is much more joyful. He is more creative. His health has improved. And he spends more time at home in his heart even when he is not in his physical home.

We want the same for you. And this is why we sound like a broken record. But know it is not broken at all. We will keep on repeating until we know you have all received our invitation. And that you have *responded* to the invitation by embodying the practices.

You might say, "How do you know? You are transmitting this book before it has even been released—before anybody has even read it." And we say we know. ☺ We can look toward a future timeline when you, and yes, we mean *you*, are reading these words. And we can see the tipping point where you get it.

And if you have gotten it already, that is wonderful. But we want *everybody* to get it. And when we say everybody, we do not limit this word to just those who read this book. We include the entire human race. We want the entire

CHAPTER 21 - THE END OF SEPARATION

human race to embrace these teachings. They are meant for all. They are not exclusive. They are not limited to people who belong to a particular religion, or a particular club, or a particular belief system. These teachings of the heart are for every human being.

These are universal teachings, my friends.

These are the teachings that were taught in one way or another by those who are known for beginning a particular religion. Yet, they never intended to start a religion! They were simply sharing universal truths much in the way we are sharing them with you. So again, we repeat, these teachings are for *all* humanity. And if there is somebody who reads these words and says, "I do not agree," that's fine. We simply encourage you to live your life and to pick the book up again whenever you feel drawn to do so.

What we seek through our teachings, friends, is to end the separation that has plagued humanity since the beginning of time, since the beginning of creation. There have been periods when there has been peace and love on your planet, but it did not last. If it had, there would be no separation today. And yet, there is.

We wish to bring you back into a state of oneness.

And we can only do that through love. There is no other way. You can talk about it and say it is the righteous thing to do. You can even say things like, "we are one." But until you know the great love within you, until you know your true self, until you know yourself as the I AM that I AM presence so strongly that all your programming and conditioning and beliefs dissolve into nothingness, there will be separation. When every man, woman, and child know themselves as they truly are, then there will be only oneness.

And so, we hope the words we transmit through this channel, and the high vibration that is inherent within them, reach as many as possible. The channel is only now just beginning to see the magnitude of this work that is being transmitted through him, the potential it has to change the world. And this is why he is here on the planet: to transmit this energy, for all to receive, to feel, and to harness.

And now, we are pushing him out of the closet, where he has hidden for much of his life. He says, "What are you talking about? I'm not hiding. I am doing a lot. ☺ I am out teaching yoga classes and offering reiki and sharing music with others." But we see him able to touch the lives of millions of people. We hope he will have the courage to share himself with the world, even if it is a bit scary at first. Blessings, dear ones.

CHAPTER 22

Slow Down

Hello, friends. We would like to ask you whether you are taking the time to close your eyes, to breathe, and to tune into your heart center *before* you read our words, as we have suggested. If it is a no, then we encourage you to start doing so. It is of great importance to put yourself into a state of receptivity in all you do in your life. And by following this guidance we offer you, you will put yourself in a state of receptivity that *really* allows you to receive our words. We encourage you not to read our words quickly, the way you are used to reading these days. But rather to read slowly.

Take your time, friends. You will receive so much more if you take your time. When you do, you will find the experience of life becomes so much more pleasurable. Right now, it is as if most of you, and we speak to society in general, are running as fast as you can on a treadmill that is moving too fast for you. And there is great struggle. You will find that if you choose to slow down, the treadmill will slow down with you, and you will come into a state of harmony. You will start to move with life at the speed you were meant to move. And your experience of life will become much more pleasurable, indeed.

Until you slow down, you will not be satisfied. Many of you think you need to speed up to get your satisfaction. It is actually quite the opposite. We are not asking you to become lazy. We are asking you to always be at rest and at ease in the present moment. And from this state of being, continue to move toward fulfilling your soul contract, the great mission you are here to fulfill. That mission is to use your gifts to anchor in this new vibration of love and light that is becoming more prevalent with every passing day. And we remind you that, even if you do not see it around you, to know that it is happening.

That is it, my friends. Slow down so you can actually enjoy the experience of life. The channel is thinking of himself moving through life in slow motion. It's kind of like that. And he gets just as much done, and even more, because he is more present to what he needs to do in the moment. We want the same for you. With great love and great light, we wish you many blessings for a nice, slow day.

CHAPTER 23

Receive the Gift

The predominant energy, dear ones, that we would like you and all of your soul brothers and soul sisters to be experiencing is to be grateful for what you have. So much unfolds when you are in a state of gratitude, in appreciation for all that you have. And this is why we are asking you to sit back, relax, and be grateful.

The ego will never be satisfied. And if it is satisfied dear ones, it will only be satisfied for short periods of time. Then, there will be another grievance, yes? Something unfulfilled. Something that is lacking. Something that is not right. *This*, you might say, is the job of the ego, to be aware of what is not working. We smile, as the channel does as well, as we speak these words through him. Because we say all of this light-heartedly with a smile on our light body faces.

So, knowing *that*, dear ones, knowing that the ego will never be satisfied for more than a moment, the practice that we offer you today is to be grateful for what you have. If you are grateful for what you have, you will feel better, yes? You will feel better in the moment. When you become receptive to all of the beauty, all of the grace, and all of the blessings that are present in your life, even if there is not a party going on in the present moment, even if there is nothing in particular that you are celebrating, you will feel better.

So, we encourage you to step into the attitude and the vibration of gratitude in each and every present moment. For you are truly blessed. If you are reading these words, you are blessed. If you are the channel speaking them, you are blessed. So be blessed, dear ones! Be grateful. Be *incredibly* grateful for what you have and be blessed.

Many of you, the channel included, are seeking *more* than you have. You all are, yes? That is the nature of the human being, to always want more. We cannot take that away from you. For it is part of your make-up to always want more. But we say to *get* it, you must be grateful for what you have in the present moment *first*. You must be in a state of gratitude.

Then, whatever it is you desire in your life will flow in a lot more *easily*. See how we stress that word *easily*? It will appear and flow towards you with more grace and more ease because you will be more *open* to it, dear ones. In a state of gratitude, you are in a state of openness, and thus you can receive. If you are not in gratitude, if you are always focused on a future that might be even better than the present moment, or if you are focused on something that you would like to have that you don't, then your energy centers will be closed. You will not be able to receive.

The channel is thinking of a silly analogy, but we will offer it regardless. He is thinking of an elevator. In a state of gratitude, the doors to the elevator are open, and whomever and whatever is meant to come into your life can come in quite easily. If you are *not* in a state of gratitude, if you are *not* grateful for what you have in the now, the doors will be closed, and nothing will get in. You understand, yes?

This is a very important teaching. It is so important and of such a high vibration that we are telling the channel that even though the book is completed, he is to insert this chapter into it in any place that he chooses. We have spoken of gratitude before, dear ones, we know. But not in *this* way. Not from *this* vibrational stance. So be grateful that you are receiving it. It is a gift. Every word that we offer you is a gift to be received with gratitude by your heart and by your spirit.

Creation itself, dear ones, is a gift. It was created for your benefit. God, that which you call the creator, birthed you as an individualized aspect of him-herself so that you might experience the gift of individual expression and the gift of *receiving* all of the bounty of the universe. You do that as an individual expression of the divine that *perceives* itself as being separate but is never actually separate from its source.

So, receive the gift, dear ones. The gift that we speak of is here for you to receive *now*. Not tomorrow. Not in a few days from now. Not in a few months or in a few years. Not when you accomplish this or that. It is here for you to receive *now*, in a state of gratitude *now*. Your lives will continue to improve if you take time to sit and to be grateful.

You are breathing, are you not? What a beautiful gift! You have a body, do you not? What an incredible gift! It is not easy to come by a body, dear ones! If you have one, you are blessed. It is a gift to have incarnated as a human being during this time of great awakening.

We are the Teachers of the Light. Many are here, joining with the channel to bring forth *our* energies for you to receive, just as the channel offers *his* loving energy as well. His knowledge, his wisdom, his life experience is offered to you as a gift so that you might learn from him and from us to be in grace and to continue to receive in a perpetual, never-ending state of gratitude.

We congratulate the channel for making himself available for this transmission. It is the strongest one (and he needs to hear this) that he has made himself available for in quite some time. And it was by choice. His spirit said it is time to make myself available for such a transmission again. It has been many months since he has done so. And his mind and his body vehicle followed and sat for longer than usual. And he once again made himself available to *us*, those who are here to support him, to guide him, and to

CHAPTER 23 - RECEIVE THE GIFT

support you and guide you as well.

And so it is, the channel will continue on this path. He will offer himself to you on a regular basis because it will be *empowering* for him to do so, and he needs to feel more empowered than he does now! He needs to feel what we would label as spiritual pride, the spiritual pride of being of service to others. And so, he will follow our guidance, and he will make himself available to you on a monthly basis now and after the book is released, which it shall be soon.

And then, he will invite you to gather around him in person. The details have not been solidified *yet*. But you will either be gathering around him in people's homes or in high-vibrational spaces that are suitable for this work and, perhaps, on retreat for a few days at a time as well. On retreat, he will not only offer meditation and channeling but his other gifts, such as music and healing.

And you will gather together, dear ones, in the name of *joy*. We will not even say it is to learn something. We will say it is to gather together in the name of joy, to be joyful together—to experience the joy of community, the joy of connecting heart to heart and soul to soul, and the joy of collaboration. For as you gather together online and in person, you will form connections by way of synchronicity that will last for many years to come. And many fruitful collaborations will come by way of these connections.

We are speaking this through the channel, so he becomes aware of what is to come. And so, all of you are on the same page! We are creating a *community* of like-minded, spiritual individuals who would like to gather together in the name of joy and in the name of creating a better planet for all of its inhabitants. And so, dear ones, we welcome you to join this community. With open arms and an open heart, we welcome you to the circle.

Perhaps some of you feel like you are outcasts. The channel has certainly always felt that way! He has always felt like an outcast—like he didn't belong. Well, perhaps, some of you feel the same way because you are a little bit different than the others, yes? It is a gift to not fit in, dear ones. It is a gift to be a little bit different. It is a gift to be unique. It is a gift to be on the fringes of society.

Do you really want to be part of society? ☺ We are making a joke, but we are also speaking candidly. So, you create your own society, yes? A society of those who consider themselves to be on the fringes. A society of those who never felt like they quite belonged.

You gather together, and you invite as many people into your community as possible. You do not have to do anything in particular to join this community that we speak of. Whoever would like to join is welcome. For all are welcome here. And together, you will create in joy. When you create in the vibration of joy, miracles become possible. For joy is one of the highest vibrations that you can experience that leads to miracles.

So *now*, we welcome you to the community. We welcome you to this sacred community. Perhaps it will have a name. We are not quite certain yet. The channel will med-

CHAPTER 23 - RECEIVE THE GIFT

itate on *that*. But we welcome you with open arms. Know that you are loved here. Know that you are accepted here. Know that you are held here—perhaps in a way that you were not as children. You are held *here*, dear ones. You are held with great love—tremendous love. We are complete.

CHAPTER 24

The Best Kind of Spirituality

Hello, friends! Perhaps you know this already simply by reading our words. But in case not, we will say it. Spirituality, what you label as spirituality, needn't be so serious all the time. We will give you an example. The channel both teaches and practices yoga. And he considers this to be a spiritual practice. And often, he will catch himself and his students with very serious faces in the poses.

From our perspective, if you have a serious look on your face, it is not the best kind of spirituality.

If you are bringing some fun and some childlike innocence into your practice, *that* is the best kind of spirituality. And so, we have mentioned this before, and we will say it again, it is time to un-adult. It is time to strip away as many of the filters as you can that have turned you into an adult. Certainly, it will be necessary to act like an adult sometimes. But it is just as necessary to act like a child sometimes, especially when it comes to your spiritual practice.

So please, bring a sense of lightness to your sacred retreats and to all of the practices we share with you in this book. And bring a sense of lightness to those we do not share with you that you are already practicing and that can be included in your bucket of spiritual practices—for there are many practices that can be labeled as spiritual. And we would actually say that every breath you take and every step you take are spiritual practices because every breath and every step *are* sacred.

The ones who we view as being most spiritual are the young children of the world.

And that is because they do not have the filters that cause them to take life too seriously. They are freer. They allow themselves to have more fun. Do you see how we bring the word *allow* back into the teaching? So, we say, *allow* yourselves to have more fun, especially in regards to your spiritual practice. If you need to push yourself to have fun, to do something your mind deems scary because it will make you feel vulnerable, then do it.

Push yourself out of the box to have fun. This is one of those rare times that we will use the word push and say that it is all right to push yourself a little bit if you are pushing yourself to have more fun. And as you still your mind and

CHAPTER 24 - THE BEST KIND OF SPIRITUALITY

move into the experience of your heart and into the experience of joy, and as you continue to enlighten, you will find it becomes easier to have more fun. And this is what we want for you. We want all of you to have more fun!

Why else would you come here if it were not to have fun? So, if you are struggling right now, know you didn't come here to struggle so much and that soon you will have more fun. You can do all you are meant to do here *while* having fun. We speak in particular of the soul contract you have come to fulfill and even the lessons you came here to learn. You can have more fun amidst it all.

We would even encourage you to put something on your calendar once a week that you consider to be a fun activity. This is the push we speak of. Many of you will say, "I don't even know how to have fun." Well then, experiment. Try different things you think might be fun until you find one that truly allows you to have a joyous child-like experience.

The channel remembers a yoga teacher who made him and his classmates make animal sounds during class. This was fun! It was a lot more fun than the traditional yoga, where some people are afraid someone will arrest them and throw them in jail if they don't get the pose perfect. ☺ It is not meant to be like that at all. And life is not meant to be like that at all, either. If you need some inspiration, look to the children. Look to see how *they* are having fun.

And we will leave you with this, friends. You need to *allow* yourself to have fun. You need to give yourself *permission* to have fun. Even when you're engaged in an activity you wouldn't normally label as fun, that you would label as serious, see what happens when you say to yourself, "I am going to allow myself to have fun right now." That might create the space for you to do something unexpected that brings a smile to your face and a smile to your heart.

We have shared many practices with you in this book. And as we journey onward, we will share more. But do not throw this one aside as if it isn't as important as the rest. It is. It is equally important as every other practice. We wish you many blessings today, friends. And we encourage both you and the channel to push yourselves to have a little more fun and to *allow* yourselves to have more fun. We can tell you we are having fun as we transmit the words through this channel. And if you come to hear us speak through the channel, you'll feel that energetically.

And so, we want to remind you that this entire life experience is meant to be an enjoyable one. And we can promise you that if you devote yourself to the practices we share with you, life will indeed become more enjoyable. Just like water will help a plant grow, our practices will help you to enjoy life. So, we say keep going. If you're not having fun right now, have faith you will soon. Have faith it is coming.

Now we have said all we need to say for today. We are laughing because very often we say goodbye to you, and we keep talking. This is just how the transmissions go very often. The channel knows by now. When we say goodbye, we do not always leave! But now, for the last time, we will say many blessings, my friends. Have fun!

CHAPTER 25

Blossom Like a Flower

Hello, friends. We are here today to remind you that the main practice, the practice around which everything else revolves, is sitting. And you must sit long enough until you smile without effort as a result of the love you're feeling in your heart.

We are over halfway through this journey together. So, in this chapter, we simply want to give you some encouragement. If you are someone who is reading these words and is very inspired, and our teachings resonate with you, but you have yet to get a taste of this great love we are speaking of, it is fine. Just continue to sit.

> *We promise you that if you continue to sit, perhaps for longer periods of time, to really still your mind, to really allow the energy to build, that in time, the love within you will begin to blossom.*

Do you see, friends, that it is impossible for a flower not to blossom? It blossoms because it is a flower, and it must. It is the divine blueprint of the flower to blossom. And it is the divine blueprint of your being for your heart to awaken and for you to experience this great love that we speak of. If you look at the flower blossoming, you will see that it does not open all at once. It opens quite slowly. There is a process by which it is nurtured by the sun, the rain, and the elements beneath it.

If you'd like, you might think of *us* as the sun, the rain, and the elements that are here to support *your* awakening. And know that if you continue to sit, if you continue to remain committed to your practice, your heart *will* awaken, and the love inside you *will* blossom. The blossoming of the love inside you is a natural unfolding of your evolution.

And we promise you that as you begin to experience the great love within you, you will know it was worth the wait, and it was worth the practice, and it was worth the time you devoted to sitting. And in fact, you will say to yourself that you were glad you did. You will say to yourself, *this* is my greatest accomplishment! That is what the channel is saying himself.

CHAPTER 25 - BLOSSOM LIKE A FLOWER

For those of you who are already there, we encourage you to invite your brothers and sisters to your home for sacred retreat. This way, there is no man, woman, or child who is left behind during this time of the great awakening. We want to see every flower blossom. For do you see the field of flowers is not complete unless every flower is open? There will come a time, we promise you, when all will have blossomed. And you will truly be living in heaven on earth, all of you.

With great love, we want you to know we are here for you. We are here for all who read these words. And we encourage you all to join the channel for his monthly online sacred retreats. We will be bringing our energy to support you during these online meditations. The channel is saying, "What? I will be doing what?" ☺ But yes, he will. That's it, my friends. Continue to blossom.

CHAPTER 26

Your Purpose for Being Here

Hello, friends. Please remember, you do not have to be in your physical home to go on sacred retreat. You can close your eyes and go on sacred retreat at your workplace or while sitting in a coffee shop. You can do it anywhere except for driving. ☺ And as we have said, when people see you in sacred retreat, and they see that smile on your face, and they feel a little more peaceful because your energy field is expanding to greet theirs, they too will rise in vibration and want to experience sacred retreat.

So, do you see, friends, that when you honor yourself and when you choose to devote yourself to practices that bring you back home into your heart, you are doing good for the world?

We are all in this together. We speak to *all* of you who are reading these words, the channel, and us, as well. We are all here with the same purpose, which is to anchor in this new high vibration of love, light, and oneness on the planet. Now is the time to remind yourself of this purpose every day. Let *it* be the motivating factor in your life. Rather than a particular goal you would like to achieve, let this purpose that you are here for be the guiding light in your life. Let it shine brightly, leading the way for you to move forward along your path in life.

> *There is great purpose for you being here on the planet right now.*

You, do you see how we stress *you*, are here to be an instrument for change. You are here to be one of the many who is creating a new paradigm on the planet. We want you to feel that, friends, and we want you to get excited about it. Why do you think you are reading this book? Why do you think you were led to it? It was not by happenstance. It was because you were meant to wake up and to know that you are here to serve this great purpose. Can you feel it *now*? Can you feel this purpose becoming alive within you? Can you feel yourself remembering who it is you are and why you are here?

- The great awakening is a great remembering.
- It is the remembering of who you are.
- It is the remembering of your divinity.

CHAPTER 26 - YOUR PURPOSE FOR BEING HERE

- It is the remembering that you are here on the planet to serve a great purpose. And this is why you have chosen to come.

The channel met with a group of people recently, and a woman asked, "What is the purpose for me being here?" And we told her what we are telling you. We told her, "You have come to experience a historic time in the evolution of humanity. You have come to experience a dimensional shift while still in physical form. You have come to experience and to help create heaven on earth. That is why you are here."

And we say the same to all of you. Let these words we speak today push you forward along your path. You know by now, we do not like to use the word push very often. But now, we will say it. Let these words excite you. Let them be the fuel that drives you. We speak only words of truth because we see the magnificence of who you are and nothing less. We see your true divinity.

The channel is laughing because his mind thought of the song "True Colors" from Cyndi Lauper. And yes, you are here to show your true colors to the world. The channel is correct when he thinks to himself this (showing your true colors) is step number three in the trilogy. You still your mind, you open your heart to the great love that is within you, and then you let it shine.

So now it is, friends, that we want you to get up in the morning and to feel *excited* about this new day that is dawning. We want you to get up in the morning and feel excited because you are part of the change that is happening. We want you to wake up excited because you know your purpose now. Maybe it was a mystery to you before, but now you know it. Perhaps you are still discovering *how* it is you will serve this purpose, through what means. But simply knowing your purpose is a good start. If it resonates with you when you go into sacred retreat, you might ask, "How may I best be of service during this great awakening? How may I best serve my purpose?" You will see; the answers will come. If not in your sacred retreat, then the universe will reflect those answers back to you.

The great awakening is an awakening of the excitement that is within you.

The channel often thinks he needs to go here or go there to experience excitement. But what we are telling *you* is that this excitement builds from within. And it comes from connecting to your purpose for being here. By now, you know what that is because we have spoken of it before, especially in this transmission. Now, we are complete.

Apparently, we are not complete. ☺ We are laughing because we want to add one more thing. When you awaken the excitement for life within you, you will awaken it within others just by being in their presence. And do not be surprised to see that more people want to be around you when you are awake in all the ways we've spoken of. OK, now we will go. We will let the channel have his oatmeal and do some gentle stretching to move prana, to awaken the life force that is within him as his day begins. Blessings, friends.

CHAPTER 27

Stilling the Mind

Hello, friends. Do you see that every thought is just a thought? You might *perceive* a thought as being very real. But how can it be? To us, and even to the channel, a thought is like a cloud in the sky. It comes; it goes.

Dear friends, you cannot take a cloud out of the sky. To try would be quite futile, yes? We are laughing. The channel is laughing, as well. He is seeing himself jumping up to the sky, trying to remove a cloud. So, we say it is OK for a thought to be there, but it is your choice as to if you let it float by, not becoming attached to it, or if you add more thoughts to that particular thought. If you do *that*, you are taking a harmless cloud, and you are turning it into a storm cloud. And then, perhaps, you will turn that storm cloud into a thunderstorm. And then, perhaps, you will add some lightning to it! ☺

Do you see what we are saying? It is OK to have the initial thought. But then, let it go. We are speaking of any thought that is not in harmony with your new high vibration. You will know right away if it is not. And you might say, "Oh, but this thought, it is very important." So, you may write it down. And then, when you enter into your sacred retreat, you may address it by asking a question about it, or praying on it, or asking for insight on it in some way. And we tell you, it will come. If not in your sacred retreat, you will still receive the answer; the universe will give it to you. It might not be that you open your eyes, step out your front door, and there it is. But you will see. Be patient, and it will be addressed.

It is only natural in a book of spiritual teachings that we take a little bit of time to address the mind. The channel himself woke up with some thoughts. We are asking him to do the same that we ask of you, to write them down if he perceives them to be important, and then let them float by. Simply by doing *that*, it is quite likely they will not need to be addressed again. But if the channel would like, he might write them down and put them aside. And in a few days from now, once these particular thoughts have drifted off, he may then return to them. And if they still feel relevant, and they might not, he might bring them into his sacred retreat in the form of questions he is seeking answers to.

CHAPTER 27 - STILLING THE MIND

Dear friends, we will tell you, as the channel knows by now, it is imperative to learn how to still your mind.

This is what children should learn in school. And it should not be an extra-curricular activity. It should be the essential practice. Do you remember we said we would talk more about the children? And here we are dropping them in here again. The channel is laughing because of the way we said that. ☺ When we said dropping, his mind thought of a child being dropped. But no, it is our intention to *tend* to the children.

There should be sacred retreat class every day for every child. And if the schools are not comfortable calling it sacred retreat, then let it be called meditation. And if they are not comfortable calling it *that*, let them call it something else. It does not matter what it is labeled for it is all the same. From day one, the children need a simple meditation practice. We feel very strongly about this. If you are a teacher, if you are in some way involved with the school system, then be courageous and bring this into every school, not only in the United States but every school everywhere.

We are not big fans of the word control. But we will say it here. And we will use the strong word *imperative* again. It is imperative that all learn how to control the mind. Now don't get the wrong idea. You do not control by forcing or pushing. It is quite the opposite. You control by sitting and softening and tuning into your breath, as you've already learned. And you do that gently, patiently, and lovingly, with a smile on your face. And then you will see the clouds come less often. And you will become much less inclined to turn a cloud into a storm cloud. And you will become much less inclined to turn *that* cloud into a thunderstorm.

Do you see that it is much more enjoyable to live under a clear blue sky, with the sun shining upon you, than to always be rained upon? If you like the rain, so be it. But we are making an analogy. Sacred retreat is the way to still your mind and to identify your thoughts for what they are outside of sacred retreat—thoughts.

We tell you, friends, this is a lifelong practice. It does not come overnight. You do not wake up one morning and find that you are a meditation master, no. The channel knows. It is only from *years* of meditation that he has cultivated a state of being that is thought-less most of the time. He knows that if a thought arises, if a thought is passing by, it is up to him what becomes of that thought. He knows it is up to him if it floats by or if he turns it into a storm cloud or if he turns it into a thunderstorm. And even *then*, he knows he is still in control of how big the storm becomes. It needn't become a hurricane. Or a tornado! ☺

You will see that when you learn to still your mind, you will have more space to use your mind for what it was meant to be used for.

Your mind is meant to align with your spirit. Your spirit

CHAPTER 27 - STILLING THE MIND

is the part of your being that knows your soul's purpose. When your mind is empty of miscellaneous thought, we will say that *divine* thought can then awaken. These are the thoughts that come from a magical place inside of you and that guide you forward along your path in life.

So, it's time, friends, for all of you to have more *magical* thoughts, the ones that arise from the divinity within you. You will quickly know when a thought is a *magical* thought because it will *feel* that way. It will get you excited. This type of thought will feel inspirational to you. You might even be so bold as to call it wisdom or insight. Do you see that insight comes from *inside* of you? It comes from inside your soul. These types of thoughts, they arise on their own, simply by being receptive, simply by being in a state of allowing, simply by way of having stilled your mind through sacred retreat, simply by resting in your heart center, all of the things that we have spoken of already.

The channel has asked, "Perhaps this chapter would have been better off earlier in the book?" But we say no. We are now going *deeper* into the mechanics of what happens once you have cultivated a daily sacred retreat practice for quite some time.

And so now it is, friends; the channel will write down the thoughts he woke up with. He labels these thoughts as worries or concerns. But then tomorrow, not today, but tomorrow, after these thoughts have had time to clear, to move on a little bit, he will sit. And it is likely he will say that some of them are no longer important. And if there is one that is, he can meditate on it, he can pray on it, and he can ask for insight about it.

This is the practice we give you today, a new practice. It is tending to your thoughts in a responsible way, tending to your thoughts in a way that brings *ease* into your life, rather than struggle.

There is one more thing the channel wishes us to address, and we will be quite specific here. There are thoughts you might have related to something you'd like to be doing in your life. The channel had a couple of those when he woke up. He thought to himself, "I wish I were at this particular awards party, wearing this particular outfit. That would be fun." And then he thought, "I wish I were having the same experience this musical artist I admire was having on YouTube at his album release party." Many of you have thoughts like this, yes? You compare yourself to others and say, "This is *my* experience, but I want *that* experience."

When you have thoughts such as these, ask yourself, what is the *feeling* I would like to experience? Let go of the comparison. Let go of it completely. Then sit in your sacred retreat. And cultivate that *feeling*, cultivate that vibration in your heart. For the channel, the words freedom, excitement, and fun come to mind. So, yes, he would cultivate the feeling of those words in his heart and just see what that leads to. It might lead to inspired action that moves him toward an *equivalent* experience. It will not be the *same* experience.

CHAPTER 27 - STILLING THE MIND

Do you see, friends, we are taking you away from creating the separation, from the jealousy, from the comparison, from the pity party. And we are moving you toward becoming empowered to tune into that higher vibration and to call it into your life experience in your own way. The channel knows it is easy to look at what somebody else is doing and think, "Oh, wow, *they* are having fun, and I'm not." Social media created this, yes? The channel has wanted us to say it for a long time: Pay less attention to it. From our perspective, it should be utilized to help people connect heart to heart and soul to soul. And *that* is it. Everything else is rubbish.

So, if you see something outside yourself that fancies you, step into your own creative power rather than allowing it to create separation and all of those other things we speak of. This is a disease of the current world. The channel's vibration means he experiences very little of it these days. For he simply sits in his high vibration and does not pay much attention to what others are doing. And we wish the same for you.

And so it is, friends; we wish you happy journeys today! And we remind you to see your thoughts for what they are. And we remind you to manifest from within, rather than focusing on what is lacking outside yourself. And we very much look forward to a day when every child is experiencing a sacred retreat as part of their schooling every day. And we ask that if you are a parent, and it is lacking in your child's school, you begin to teach it in your home. Not only to your child but to other children, too. And if you do not feel as if *you* are equipped to teach it, then have somebody who is equipped come to your house to teach it.

Friends, you will see a noticeable difference in your children fairly quickly because they pick it up faster than adults. And if it becomes manifest in the way we would like it to become manifest, you will see less violence among your children. This is a big one, yes?

This is a heated conversation, politically speaking—when we speak of the gun violence in the United States. But we say that sacred retreat will help. And prior to the end of this book, we will offer some additional insights for the children, as well. Many blessings, my friends.

CHAPTER 28

Higher, Higher, Higher

Dear friends, if you get to know the channel in person or virtually, you will see that he is a very humble man. And so it is, he wants you to know that he is on the same journey that you are on. He is on the same journey of raising his vibration. He is on the same journey of truly knowing himself as a light being. By way of his soul contract and his purpose here on the planet, he has a very sincere desire to elevate you through the words that are transmitted through him and by his presence. He is not shy about telling you he too has risen through the mud like a lotus flower into the light, and now he is continuing to rise higher, and higher, and higher. And with much love in his heart, he is here to assist you to do the same.

The channel *himself* will look back in a few years from now, and he will no longer experience himself as the same person he is right here and right now in this chair as he transmits these words. Because his vibration, too, is still rising higher. This is the natural evolution of humanity. Just as there is a seed that contains an infinite intelligence that turns into a fully blossomed tree, there is an infinite intelligence within all of you that is guiding you forward toward your evolution as a human race so that you may come to experience yourselves as the light beings you are, and so you may all rise to the highest vibration possible.

This is the journey you, the channel, and all of humanity are on right now. And what a fun journey, we say. And we say that you are all here for this adventure, for the evolution of your own species. It is happening now. So, celebrate your own awakening. Rejoice in your own awakening as it occurs. And wherever it is you are vibrationally today, be OK with it.

Fairly recently, the channel read a book transmitted by another channel. And the particular energies that were transmitting through this channel encouraged its readers to speak three words quite often, "Raise, raise, raise." These are good words. But we would encourage you to say the words, "Higher, higher, higher." Because that is where you are going—to a higher level of consciousness, to a higher vibration, and to a much more pleasurable experience of life.

CHAPTER 28 - HIGHER, HIGHER, HIGHER

And *remember* why you are here. It is not only for the adventure and awakening, but it is to assist all humanity to rise. So, when you see somebody struggling because they are experiencing a lower vibration because their frequency is not as high as yours, you have a responsibility to lift them up rather than ignore them. And then, your purpose is complete. We will leave you with *that*. But know that these two sentences we have just transmitted are very important. So, you might read them multiple times. And then you can say, "Ah yes, *that* is why I am here on the planet." Blessings, friends.

CHAPTER 29

Stay High

Hello, friends. As always, it is with great love in our hearts that we greet you. For we want to remind you, it is a wonderful time to be alive. We want to remind you it is a time to be excited about being here and serving your purpose on the planet during this great time of awakening for humanity.

It is true what they say. History does not repeat itself. And so, this great awakening will not repeat itself in the same way that it is happening *now*! Celebrate every moment of it and your participation in it. Rejoice! Because now is the time you have waited for. Many of you have had many other experiences that have led to having this particular experience. And when we say many other experiences, we refer to other expressions of the divine that *you* chose. Because you knew your experience as those expressions would be fruitful for participating in the great awakening that is happening *now,* and that you are part of *now,* and the particular form of the divine that you are expressing and being *now*.

> *You might even say that everything has led up to this moment, to this historic time of awakening that you are participating in by choice.*

You wanted to be part of it. You wanted to be part of the celebration happening now. The channel is beginning to feel that excitement well up from within. A reminder: It doesn't well up from outside of yourselves. It comes from your spirit, from the knowing of why you are here. And if you focus too much attention on what is around you, then you might easily forget that purpose. And the excitement that is already within you, waiting to awake, might not have the opportunity to awaken.

If you are focusing too much of your awareness on what is around you, and you feel stuck in the same vibration you were in when you began reading this book, it is time to spend more time going within and awakening from within. We have told you many different times, in many different ways, *this* is the path of awakening. It is the path to awakening the excitement within you. It is the path to awakening *everything* that is inside you. You must go within.

And this is the problem plaguing humanity. As a whole, you are spending too much time focusing your awareness on the outside world as opposed to spending more time going within yourselves.

Going within is the key that will unlock the door to everything you want to experience in your life.

And for those who have chosen to take this journey of awakening, we and the channel are here to fully support you. If you have a question, you may reach out to the channel, and he will reply. We, the Teachers of the Light and the channel himself, are here to support your awakening. That is our purpose on the planet.

And so, we ask you, "What is *your* purpose on the planet?" We already know the answer. It is to do the same for others in your own way, in the way *you* are meant to. For every step you take, there will be many people who need you to reach out your hand and lift them up to the step you're on. And it is by doing *this* that you fulfill your purpose here on the planet. And it is by doing *this* that you will see you are filled with *real* satisfaction.

Do you notice how we highlight the word real? We are not talking about fleeting satisfaction that comes and goes because you experience a temporary pleasure in the outside world. We are talking about *real* satisfaction, the kind of satisfaction that fills your heart and soul with joy. You experience that joy because you are serving your purpose on the planet by assisting others in this time of great awakening.

We have one purpose, and again we speak of both ourselves and the channel, and that is to uplift you. And so it is, these words we speak contain a vibration that will help to uplift you. But you must uplift yourself, as well, by choosing to do so.

> *You have been given free will, friends, and you can use that free will to uplift yourself and to uplift others.*

You can use your free will in many different ways. It is a free-will zone! So, if you choose, you may use your free will for other purposes. But we say that *this* is why you were given free will: So that you may choose to participate in this great awakening in the highest way possible. We have to repeat it. It is happening; it is happening; it is happening. No matter what it is you see with your naked eyes, know that you cannot see all that is happening beneath the surface. And it is happening; it is happening; it is happening!

Change is occurring right here and right now for the highest good of humanity. Because, as we have said many times, everything is happening in divine order. It is happening as it should. We have no other purpose in this particular transmission except to get you excited and to help you awaken to the excitement within you.

Do not allow your own personal vibration to sink down to the vibration of others, friends. Use your free will to keep *your* vibration high. If somebody else has a low vibration, do your best to uplift them. And if they are open to

CHAPTER 29 - STAY HIGH

being helped, as many will be, then you help them. And if not, then so be it. They will find the way. But no matter what, make it a priority to maintain your own high vibration. Make it a priority to get excited from within.

You must be diligent about where you place your attention in the world. You have every right to place your attention on things that make you feel good vibrationally and that get you excited. If you do *that* and you spend a lot of time awakening from within yourself, all will be well. The power is within you to maintain your own high vibration and to continue to raise it.

You do not have to waste your time doing as some others are doing. You do not have to give your awareness away to any news that brings you down. You do not have to spend time with people who bring you down. You do not have to engage in any form of social media that lowers your vibration. You can make a difference in the world by staying high.

Stay high, my friends. That is what we are encouraging you to do. You do *that* by awakening from within and selectively choosing where you place your awareness in the outside world. And if you are to say to us, "Oh, but Teachers of the Light, I am in a low vibrational experience that I cannot get out of. There is no way out." We say the way out is by awakening from within. Then, the way out will reveal itself to you. You will see, as you raise your vibration, as you take responsibility for *that*, there will be a way out. And then, a new higher vibrational experience will come into your life.

Dear ones, if you find that you have difficulty embodying this particular teaching on your own and that the vibration we share in these words is not supportive enough, then call upon your brothers and sisters for help. There are many lightworkers available now who can lift you up and teach you how to experience heaven on earth. Now is the time to live your purpose. Now is the time to experience the life you came here to experience. Now is the time to *fully* participate in the great awakening that is at hand. It is now; it is now; it is now.

Many of you think you have all the time in the world to awaken. And it is quite a paradox. Because on the one hand, you do. There is no end, friends. So, if it takes you a billion more incarnations, a billion more expressions, to awaken to the light within you, that is OK. But we say, don't delay. We say awaken now. Many of you have delayed long enough. Awaken *now* and participate fully *now* in this great awakening.

Join the party, friends!

There is no need to observe it from the outside. Be part of it. Be part of the celebration. Use your uniqueness to contribute to it. The channel was feeling a little bit dreary this morning. His mind was a little grumpy. But *now*, he is feeling it. *Now*, he is feeling the excitement welling up from inside himself. And we believe you are as well. The words

CHAPTER 29 - STAY HIGH

we speak are powerful, and they have a vibration inherent within them that is meant to lift you into your rightful place in the kingdom of heaven. Please know, friends, there is no religious context whatsoever in those words. There is no religion *here*. These teachings are universal. They are at the *root* of all true religion, not just one.

And actually, there is only one religion that is meant for all humanity to experience. It is the religion of love, which leads to the experience of oneness. And that, my friends, is not a religion at all. It is simply fulfilling your highest potential as a human race. There will be a time when most religions will fade away. And when we say that, we mean religion in the forms you have come to know. The rituals in the religions will be alive and well and flourishing as they have never flourished before. And all will be invited to participate in these rituals. They will not be rituals where only a few are chosen to participate. You will be invited *regardless* of whether you belong to a particular group. We are moving into the time when *all* belong.

Celebrate. Celebrate *now*. Awaken *now*. Now is the time. Feel it in the depths of your soul and know it is true. And know that the truth comes from within you. Our words simply *trigger* the truth that is already within. And that is how you know, friends, if the teaching is true, if it resonates as true within *yourself*. If it does not, that is perfectly fine. You can donate the book to a charity. ☺ Or give it to a friend. But if the words we speak and the vibration inherent within them resonates with your spirit, then we very much look forward to continuing this journey of awakening with you.

Blessings, friends. Please know we have great love for you. We wish for you to close your eyes, to relax, to soften, to allow, and to receive this great love we have for you. The love that is had for you is beyond your belief. The channel is only now beginning to experience it because he has opened up to it. And as he experiences it, his mind says, "Oh, wow, this is wonderful. I like it." And he will only experience more of it as his journey continues.

We want you to experience it as well. And so that is why we ask you to close your eyes, to soften, to allow, and to receive. And that is why we encourage you to join the channel as we share our energies with you in all the ways we will be doing, both in-person and virtually. Thus, you will feel uplifted. You will receive the support you want and need at this historic time of awakening.

We are the Teachers of the Light, and we shine our light upon you in support of your awakening. We would like every human being to experience the love we have for them and the love and light that is within them. Now is the time to spread this message of love and light to all. Now is the time. It is happening. It is happening. It is happening now.

CHAPTER 30

Your Garden of Gifts

Hello, friends. All of you have unique gifts to share with the world. And as we have stated, it is very likely these gifts are related to your purpose; they are related to what we have labeled as your soul contract. Who is it who must nurture these gifts? It is you, of course.

You already know what your gift, or for many of you, what your gifts are, yes? So, we encourage you to choose the ones you would like to nurture. To us, we see that each of you has a beautiful garden of gifts, and you must choose which of these gifts you will water. In the previous chapter, we said that now is the time. So now we will add a few words to *that*. Now is the time to let your light shine. And for some of you, that means it is time to nurture your gifts, to tend to them in the way a gardener might tend to a garden.

Some of you make every excuse in the world for not nurturing your gifts. The most common one, of course, is, "I do not have time. I am too busy." How is it, friends, that you could be too busy to live your purpose if that is what you came here to do? We say there is time. We say there are things you are doing that are a waste of time and that are not *absolutely* necessary to do in your life. You know what these things are.

Take away these things, and there will be time. Even if you are tending to children, even if you are tending to a job that has no purpose other than to sustain yourself financially, we say you can find little cracks during the day to nurture your gifts if you make that a priority.

For some of you, this chapter is completely unnecessary because you are already tending to your gifts in the way you are meant to. It is likely you are serving your purpose by expressing yourself using those gifts. But for others, you have not paid attention to them. And it is time. Many of you say, "Oh, *tomorrow*, there will be more time to tend to my gifts."

Dear ones, now is the time.

For a moment, we will speak candidly regarding the form you are in. It is disposable, yes? And you only get one walk-through in this particular form. You get the point without our needing to elaborate it, yes? So, my friends, every now and then, it is good to face your own mortality

CHAPTER 30 - YOUR GARDEN OF GIFTS

as a *human* being. And to utilize *that* as motivation to tend to your gifts *now*. If there is something you would like to do, do it now.

Perhaps this chapter, more so than any other chapter, comes from a more physical point of view. Do you see what we are saying? For you are in a physical world, are you not? Now is the time to fully anchor the greatness of your spirit into *it* and to express the greatness of your spirit through your physical form. Now is the time to truly be the creative being you are.

Find the time. That will create some momentum, friends. That momentum will create some increased motivation. And you will see that naturally, things begin to flow. Naturally, you will begin to feel more excited about your life. If you are not feeling very excited, why do you think that is? It is because you are not nurturing your gifts. You are not honoring your soul contract. You are not fulfilling your purpose. With tough love, we say now is the time to do *that*.

You might feel that energetically, the vibration of these words is coming from a different space. And that is the case. This will be the one *physical* push we give you. We will give you an example from the channel's life. He has some aspirations to use the gifts he has as a musician to touch the hearts and souls of more people. That is part of his soul contract. He is diligent about tending to his gift. He is diligent about nurturing it. He is disciplined. And yet, *he* could use a little push. Instead of practicing for an hour a day, he could do two. He could push himself a little more. That is what we are saying. And we share this with you because some of you can do the same. And you know who you are. You are saying, "Yes, yes, yes! I agree. This is relevant for me."

So, you might say, dear friends, this particular teaching is the one meant to light a fire in your belly, to ignite a spark within you that says, "Yes, I will find the time to nurture my gifts and to push myself to share them with the world as I am meant to." We have said we do not like the word push. But in this context, we will use it because it's appropriate.

Push does not mean you have lost anything that you gained from any of the other practices we have shared with you. In fact, we would say they are the *foundation* for *this* particular teaching.

It is likely that many of you are in the process of mastering all our teachings simply by practicing them. And so now we wish you to master this teaching, as well.

Dear friends, we only want the best for you. And that is why we share this particular teaching with you. We want to offer you something that is very grounded in what you call your reality. But please know this does not take away from any of our other teachings. And we will put all our other teachings into a few simple sentences now to remind you of them. We do so because the channel is a little afraid people will read this particular transmission and forget all about our other essential teachings.

CHAPTER 30 - YOUR GARDEN OF GIFTS

You know by now there is a great love within you. And when you connect to this love through sacred retreat and through all of our other teachings, you will find yourself elevated to a state of consciousness in which you feel a much greater sense of peace, contentment, and even bliss and ecstasy.

And this state of being, this state of consciousness, is not related to the teaching in this particular chapter. It is not related to the push we spoke of. In fact, you could ignore this chapter altogether and just focus on cultivating this state of being, and you would be fine. But even so, there would be a little piece of your mind that circles back and says, "I do not feel *completely* satisfied." The mind will say *that* if you are not tending to your gifts and sharing them with the world in the way you are meant to.

So, we say now is the time to have it all.

That is the teaching for today, friends. Now is the time to have it *all*—the peace, the contentment, the bliss, and the ecstasy that come from the spiritual practices, as well as the satisfaction that comes from nurturing your gifts and sharing them with the world in a purposeful way. Put those together, and the journey is complete. Your destiny is fulfilled. And then the body can discard itself at the proper time. And your spirit can journey onward to the next adventure. We do hope, friends, that you feel inspired on *all* levels. And we wish you many blessings for a day in which you experience *everything* you have come here to experience. Now is the time. Let it happen. Blessings, friends.

CHAPTER 31

Vibrational Shifting

Hello, friends. You have been practicing sacred retreat for some time now, yes? So, you know that very often, you might begin your sacred retreat not feeling as high as you would like to, vibrationally speaking. But when you open your eyes after your sacred retreat, you feel uplifted, don't you? Your mind is quiet, and your vibration is higher.

And so it is, friends; now we want to introduce you to a new practice that is called vibrational shifting. You have been practicing this for some time already. Because every time you go into sacred retreat, you shift vibrationally. Every time you go into sacred retreat, you rise a little higher. Yet, you are having a human experience. And sometimes you might wake up and say to yourself, as the channel did this morning, "I feel grumpy. I feel depressed. I have a headache." The prescription that we offer you is to sit in sacred retreat for as long as you need to experience a vibrational shift, to sit as long as you need until you feel uplifted—until you are high again.

There is no reason to stay low. Now you have a practice that enables you to *shift* quickly. Do you see, friends, that once you've practiced sacred retreat twice a day for an extended period of time, you will have raised your vibration considerably? And even when your vibration drops, you are well equipped to raise it again very quickly. You might only need to sit for five or ten minutes during the day when you feel low to uplift yourself back to the high vibration you seek to be in.

By way of your twice-daily sacred retreat, you have given yourself an invaluable tool you can use at any time during the day to lift, to raise, and to get back to the place you belong, dimensionally speaking.

You do not have to stay away from home for a very long time. Home is your new high vibration. And as part of that new high vibration, your heart is open so that the creator's love within you might shine through for all the world to see and experience. Do you see, friends, you have the power within you to uplift yourself and to raise your vibration now at will? This is the greatest tool you gave to yourself through your practice.

Now, do you see why the sacred retreat instruction came very early and why this chapter comes quite late? There is a natural progression to these teachings you must follow. Some won't follow the progression, and nothing will hap-

CHAPTER 31 - VIBRATIONAL SHIFTING

pen. They must go to the beginning and commit to a daily sacred retreat practice before they enable themselves to do these mini-vibrational shifts.

The channel did it for himself this morning because he needed one. But it is available to you anytime and anywhere. It needn't be in your home. It could be where you work or when you're out with people who sometimes take you out of your high vibrational home. This is your tool; it is what you carry with you so that you may stay high as often as possible.

We wish you many blessings during your day and encourage you to stay high. Even if others are low, there is no reason to join them. And when you are feeling low, there is no reason to stay there for a very long time. The power is within you to lift yourself up to a higher vibration. And if you are not quite there yet, meaning if this particular teaching seems a little beyond you, and you can't experience this shift, that is fine. Be patient. Be loving toward yourself. With practice, it will come. It simply means you need to continue your sacred retreat practice.

And if you need support, the channel is here to help you. Even if you need to send him an email to simply get some support, through words that come from him and not us, he is available for that. Both we, the Teachers of the Light and the channel, are here to support you, to lift you up, and to help you to experience all that is possible for you to experience in this incarnation.

And dear ones, if you do notice you are feeling low on a particular day, and perhaps it is you don't even know why, you needn't take it as an opportunity for the mind to complain and say, "Oh, I was so high yesterday, but today I am low." Do you see that a thought such as this one will only continue to lower your vibration? It is like throwing more wood into the fire.

Simply notice what's happening, without judgment, without allowing your mind to become involved. In fact, if anything, celebrate and say to yourself, "How wonderful, I have noticed. I am a little lower today than I was yesterday." And then decide to sit and to raise. Perhaps you will sit, and you will raise quite a bit, but you may not raise again as you did the day prior. Again, you needn't judge *that*. Avoid the traps that many people fall into by way of the mind. Blessings, dear ones.

CHAPTER 32

Embrace the Change

Dear ones, as you take this journey with us and with your brothers and your sisters who are also reading these words, it is inevitable that at some time during the journey, you will feel a pull from within to make a change in your life. And that pull comes because your inner being knows there is an experience to have that is a better vibrational match for who it is you have become and who it is you are becoming.

And so, you might wake up on a particular day and say, "Oh yes, now is the time to make a change so that I might match up with this new experience." We simply invite you to make it, to let go of the resistance, and to allow it to happen. If you fight it, it is likely you will create suffering in your life. If you resist it, you might create a battle between your mind resisting the change and your spirit, which is leading you in a particular direction. So, simply let go and flow and embrace the change; it is a natural part of life.

The channel has often thought to himself, "The only constant in life is that it is always changing." And so it is, on occasion, you will feel pulled from deep within to make bigger changes in your life. Celebrate them. It means you have graduated from one particular vibration, and now you are moving on to the next.

This is even how we see the death of the human body. Many people know it is time, and they fight *that*. And thus, they create unnecessary suffering for themselves. Or it could be that a loved one does not want the person to go. And so, *they* actually create unnecessary suffering for the one who is leaving because they do not give them permission to leave the body when it is time.

If you look back upon your lives from this present moment, you will see that when you *resisted* change, you created unnecessary suffering in your lives. And *that* is fine. It is not something to become judgmental about, but it is good to note. So, when the next time comes around, you will let go of your resistance, and you will allow your inner being to move you to the next experience that is waiting for you.

If there is upheaval going on in your life right now because there is a big change that is happening, then celebrate that. For it means you are moving to a higher vibrational experience. And it is your spiritual practice that allows you to move through it with grace and with ease.

CHAPTER 32 - EMBRACE THE CHANGE

You will find that even the biggest of changes can be quite easeful if you have been committed, and you continue to commit to your spiritual practice. Then even the biggest of changes will be like a walk through the park because you will be connected to the peace within you.

By now, you have cultivated a state of being through your sacred retreat that allows you to move through transitions with more grace and ease. And that is another gift the practice of sacred retreat offers you.

We will say this, friends, because it is a good analogy. If you were to take two people, and they were each going through a major life transition because their inner being was calling them to a higher vibrational experience (that requires letting go of an old one), the person with a daily sacred retreat practice will find the transition much easier than the person without one.

We will leave you with *this*. There are a few of you out there who are reading our words, but that's all you're doing. You are reading them, and you are enjoying them, and you are saying, "Oh yes, I agree with this." But you have yet to *practice*. You will get very little out of simply reading the words. But you will get so much out of practicing. That is how you raise your vibration. That is how you experience the kingdom of heaven within you. And again, we remind you that we do not say that in a religious context. These are universal teachings meant for all.

So, it is friends, if you happen to be one of those few who aren't practicing, go back to the beginning and actually incorporate the practices into your life. Then, you can get back to this chapter. And you will feel quite different than you do now. That is all we have to share with you today, friends. For those of you who are experiencing change in your lives because the great awakening is a time of great change, we encourage you to allow it to happen and to celebrate as you raise, raise, raise and thus experience more adventures that align with your new high vibration.

CHAPTER 33

Love, Strength, and Power

Hello, friends. As you know by now, we are advocates of awakening to the great love and the great light within you. For from our perspective, these are the two qualities of the creator that are most important. In fact, without these two qualities of love and light, there would be no creation. You would not be here as you are.

Everything is created from love. Everything returns to love, as well. And it is only by way of your mind, and your programming, and your conditioning that at times you feel separate from it and separate from your source, which is love. And so now you see why we are advocates of love. If you only come to know one quality of the creator, then let it be love.

But we are here to remind you that every quality inherent in the creator is inherent in you. It can be no other way. On this particular day, the channel is feeling strength and power. In other words, he is feeling the presence of the creator within him in a new way. And he is saying to himself, "Oh yes, this is me, too. I am not only love, but I am great strength. I am great power."

And so it is, my friends; this teaching is very simple. It is to remind you of what you know already, of what it is you know already in your spirit, that whatever the creator is, you are also. If the creator is love, you are that, too. If the creator is strength, you are strength. If the creator is power, then you are power. And we do not speak of the egotistical kind of power; we speak of the benevolent kind, the kind that gives you confidence to create for the benefit of all.

Even humor is a quality of the creator. How could it not be? For it is within you as well. It is within us, the Teachers of the Light. It is within the channel; it is within all. The gentleness a mother displays toward her child is another quality of the creator.

Now is the time to come to know yourself as the creator knows him-herself. As you enlighten, you only let go of what is *not* the creator. You do not let go of any of the good stuff. You only let go of what is holding you back from knowing yourself fully and completely as the god-self you are. And at the same time, you make space for more of your god-presence to become embodied in your physical form so that all of you is present.

Do you see, friends, that this is the purpose of your existence—to anchor your god-self fully and completely in your physical form? And it is possible, very possible indeed.

CHAPTER 33 - LOVE, STRENGTH, AND POWER

Many have done this on your planet. Many more will. It is likely you will be one of them if you are not yet. Then, you are whole, and you are complete because you lack nothing. You are everything that you are. This is how you actually are already. It is simply remembering.

So today, perhaps you will invite yourself to feel the strength and power within you. Perhaps, you will invite yourself to feel these qualities of the creator that are within you or any other qualities of the creator you wish to experience today.

Remember, friends, you are not seeking to bring anything that is outside yourself into yourself. You are simply seeking to bring more of yourself into your present form. Do you see the difference? It is a very important difference.

We speak of these two qualities today because they are quite important for many of you. When you are connected to, and when you are experiencing those qualities that are within yourself, you feel more confident. You have a greater sense of knowing that you can indeed accomplish whatever it is you want to accomplish. You can go out into the world, and you can move toward your dreams, whatever they are, knowing the power is within you to manifest them.

You will see the energy of this transmission is a little bit different from our other ones, yes? You might even say it is a little more action-oriented. When we speak of going out into the world and accomplishing what you are meant to accomplish, that is, of course, related to your soul mission during this time of great awakening.

All our teachings go hand in hand. There are none that

contradict each other. But we do want our teachings to be complete and whole. That is why we bring this transmission to you today. While it is no less important than any of our other teachings, it, too, comes later. Because if you are experiencing the strength and power of the creator within you, but have yet to experience the great love and light within you, then your strength and power will be misguided.

You see this happening all around you, correct? There are many who do not have much of a problem knowing their strength and their power. But they have not taken the time to connect to the great love within them. And that is most important. Unless you have that, you will have no good place to direct your strength and your power in the world. So, love is first. Do you see how incredibly important this teaching is? Do you see how we seek to bring everything back into balance?

Every man and woman should be loving. And they should know the strength and the power that is within them to express that love for the benefit of everyone. This is the teaching. It is an incredibly important lesson, and that is why we are saying it again. Those who know love can come to know the strength and the power that is within them quite easily. But it can be more challenging for those who do not know love but only know strength and power to see beyond their strength and power so they may know love and then integrate their strength and power with their love to be of service in the world. We wish there to be balance in the world in every way possible.

CHAPTER 33 - LOVE, STRENGTH, AND POWER

The channel is asking us what we can do (when he says we, he refers to himself and those who are reading these words) to help others achieve a balance of love, strength, and power. And we are going to say it simply. If you know somebody who is very loving, but they are not aware of their strength and power, simply reflect that (the strength and power that is within them) back to them. Say to them, "I see you as being strong and powerful." And they will say to themselves, "Wow!" And those simple words will help them experience this aspect of themselves.

It might be a little more challenging if somebody is out of balance because they only know their strength and power, but they do not know the love. These are the ones who need to be softened with gentle love. So, we say, friends, just do your best to love them and say, "There is a part of you that is very loving and nurturing. It will be wonderful to see this part of you manifest itself."

And so it is, we encourage you to know all of yourself, not just bits and pieces. Remember, it is all within you already. You simply need to know what parts of yourself you need to tend to more. And then you tend to those aspects of yourself, much in the way you would tend to a garden. There might be a particular plant that needs a little more attention. It is like this. That is it for today. We wish you many blessings. And whatever part of the creator you need more of, know that it is within you. And simply by tending to it, you will experience more of it. Blessings.

CHAPTER 34

Vibrational Awareness

Hello, friends. There are people and environments that make you feel very good, and there are others that make you feel not so good, yes? This is because every person and every environment is emitting a frequency, a vibration. And *your* vibration is either in harmony with that vibration, or it is not. And if there is harmony, it will feel quite pleasing, and you will want to spend more time with that person or in that environment. And if there is not, well then you won't feel good, and you will want to walk away!

We are sharing this with you so you can become vibrationally aware. And thus, you will know quite quickly what is a good fit for you and what is not. And so it is, you might meet a particular person, and their vibration matches your vibration. And you might say to yourself, "Oh, this is a person I want to spend more time with." Perhaps, they're a friend, or a romantic partner, or a colleague. We encourage you to gravitate, as best you can, toward the people and the environments that *are* a vibrational match for you. In this way, you are activating your power as a creator. You are saying yes to *this* and no to *that*.

And if you notice you are in the company of a particular person or in an environment that is not suitable vibrationally, it never means you need to lower your vibration to meet theirs or to meet that particular environment. You stay high.

And we tell you that by staying high, one of three things will happen. Either the particular person, group of people, or environment that was not a match for you will become more of a match for you (this is the power of your vibration—this is the power of love). Or it will drop away. Or there will be a way out. It might not happen instantaneously, but you will see it is likely to happen. And by activating your power as a creator in *that* way, by staying high in vibration, you will see a new experience come along that is a better match for you. This is the law of attraction at work in every way. It is all vibration.

CHAPTER 35

Suffering

Dear friends, there is a sacred prayer the channel enjoys reciting. It is "Lokah Samastah Sukhino Bhavantu." It translates as, "May all beings everywhere be happy and free. May my own thoughts and words and actions contribute to the happiness and well-being of all."

There is suffering on the planet, correct? At times you may find that *you* are the one suffering. And thus, every practice we have shared with you is a practice that will help to *relieve* your own suffering. Often, you might see another who is suffering. There is nothing wrong with feeling empathy. There is nothing wrong with feeling compassion. These are good qualities to have. But the best way to be of service is just to hold this particular person in the highest light possible.

What we mean is that when you see somebody who is suffering, do your best to stay anchored in the high vibration of love. Simply by doing *that*, you will relieve their suffering a little bit. The channel does this when somebody who is suffering sees him for reiki. Rather than buying into their story and going on the ride with them, he holds the high space of love. And simply by way of this vibration, the other person may come into resonance with this love, and they are uplifted.

So, when you see someone who is suffering, we invite you to do the same thing as the channel. See the godliness in them. It is no different from the godliness within you. And then act out of love, not out of pity. If you are acting out of love, there will likely be words to exchange. You might say, "I see the strength, the power, and the godliness within you. I see you as who you are. And I reach out my hand in love, brother or sister, to assist you in any way I can."

Do you see how incredibly powerful that is, friends? And do you see it is a much more pleasurable experience to do *that* while you are staying high in the vibration of love as opposed to getting hooked into their story? That will do no good for either of you. But you have great power to transform others through love by thinking and acting from this high vibrational space of love.

In part, we are responding to something a woman inquired about at a group channeling last night. She said, "I feel very sad when I see others who are suffering. What can I do?" This is our response: You do not need to ponder *why* another person is suffering, meaning you do not need to ask why them and not me. And you do not even need to ask when it is the other way around, why me and not them. That is all mind-stuff. You simply need to be in love.

The channel is asking, "Is it not important to know why I am suffering, so I can change?" We are saying, yes, that can be helpful. But do not compare yourself to someone else. If you are the one who is suffering, and you feel like it would be beneficial to know why, then you might ask yourself, "Why am I suffering?" And perhaps you will know quite quickly. And that will allow the space for you to change.

And we will leave you with this, friends. If you are devoting yourself to the practices, and you still feel as if your vibration is not shifting (and to us, this is what we call suffering), that means you cannot do it alone, and *that* is fine. It means it is time to reach out, to get assistance to help you raise your vibration.

We are all here to help each other. We are all here to assist each other during this great awakening. We are all here to support each other. We are all here to help each other raise our individual vibrations so that the global collective consciousness can continue to raise even higher and so that all may reside in love and have the experience of residing in heaven on earth.

So, if you need help, do not be afraid to ask for help. Help will be given. But we say you must devote yourself to the practices in this book for quite some time. And if you do, there *will* be a shift. You will elevate yourself. And thus, you will know the great power within you to do so. And then, if you need a little bit of extra assistance, that is fine. We, the channel and the Teachers of the Light and many other light workers are all here to assist. That is it for today, friends. Blessings.

CHAPTER 36

There Is Greatness Inside You

Dear friends, this will be a short transmission. The channel had an experience recently when he did something new that he wishes to excel in. And afterward, he said, "Oh, I didn't do it very well. Perhaps I'll give up."

Do you see that when you do something new, it is very likely because you have a gift for it because it relates to your soul's purpose? And just because it does not go as intended, just because it does not live up to *your* expectations the first time out, does not mean it is time to give up. It means you need to continue to tend to the gift until you excel at it.

There are many people who did not have much talent in a particular area. And we are not speaking of you, the readers. ☺ Still, they continued to tend to it because they felt very strongly it was their purpose to share this gift with others. By way of their devotion, they tended to a gift so that it flourished beautifully. You can do the same with all *your* gifts. You just need to observe the nature of the ego that might say, "Oh, I am not good at this. So, I will give it up." That is just your mind. If you are going to excel at something, you must devote yourself to it until you master the craft. Never give up too easily.

If you are going to give up, let it be for good reason. Let it be because you feel inspired to do something else, not because you are listening to your mind-stuff that says you are not good enough. Do you see the difference? There is greatness inside all of you. So, continue to tend to this greatness. And you will see it flourish and expand, and you will be happy you chose to devote yourself to tending to your gift or your gifts. That's it for today, friends.

CHAPTER 37

Nonjudgment

Hello, friends. This will be another short transmission. By way of our other teachings, it is quite likely you are aware of this already. But yet, we say it again just in case. There is never any need to judge your sacred retreat practice as being a good one or a bad one. In fact, for the purpose of sacred retreat, get rid of those words (good and bad). It is a practice.

Your experience of sacred retreat will not always be the same. If you sit down for a sacred retreat one day, and you notice your mind is more active than it was during another sacred retreat, that is fine. Do not take it as an opportunity to judge yourself or to judge your sacred retreat practice.

Do you see, friends, that when you look up to the sky on any given day, it is likely there will be more or fewer clouds than were there the day before? Your thoughts are like these clouds, and it will be like this during your sacred retreat practice. Some days will have more clouds than other days. And that is fine.

But what you will see, as you progress with this practice, is that there will be more days with fewer clouds. That will be the result of your practice. But always remember that it is a practice. It isn't something you can get right or wrong. And you are not practicing for something. You are not practicing for a future event. You are practicing for the moment of practice. And by practicing for the sake of practicing, your experience of sacred retreat will continue to become more pleasurable. That is it for today, friends.

CHAPTER 38

Keep Going

Dear ones, we wish to speak about fear. Perhaps this is one of the most common human experiences. Where we reside, there is no fear. There is only love. You might say that there is so much love that fear cannot even exist. And that is why as you raise your vibration through sacred retreat and the other practices, you will feel less of it. You will be more absorbed in love.

Do you see how it works, friends? The more love you feel, the less fear you will have. But we wish to tell you that fear is not always a bad thing. For in the reality you are participating in, the Earth plane, it might be that you are feeling some fear because you are about to step into something new. Simply step forward anyway. The fear is not a sign that tells you to turn around. It is a sign that is saying you are about to step into uncharted waters. And you are about to do that because you are courageous and because you have come to the planet to take chances.

We are using whatever the channel is experiencing this evening to bring forth this teaching for you, friends. He, too, is feeling a little fear because *he* is about to step into something new. But it is a good thing. There are no lions, tigers, or bears chasing him. ☺ So, be honest with yourself about where your fear is coming from. Most of the time, it will be coming from a place within you that is weary of stepping forward into the unknown.

And then you step forward, and the fear dissipates, and you get to experience something new.

The channel often likes to think of fear as false expectations appearing real. And you may do the same if it pleases you and if it helps you to put fear in its rightful place. Celebrate it, friends. Rejoice if you are feeling it. It is likely a guidepost that excitement is about to occur.

We also want to say that all of those whom you look up to, your mentors and your teachers, are not experiencing what they are experiencing today because they never felt any fear. They are experiencing what they are experiencing today because when they felt the fear, they acknowledged it, and they stepped through it to the other side.

And occasionally, or perhaps even many times, they tripped, and they fell. Things did not go exactly as they had hoped. Yet, they kept on going. Today, these particular people are people who are well-known for what they do. But by no means ever compare yourself to anybody else.

CHAPTER 38 - KEEP GOING

You are on your own unique journey. If you look to a mentor or a teacher for inspiration, that is all right. Only the ego compares.

What we are getting at, friends, is that if you want to expand, if you want to live the greatest life *you* can live, if you want to express yourself in your unique way, the way *you* were meant to, then see fear for what it is, not as a stop sign but rather as a guidepost that says, "How exciting! Keep going." If you do *that*, friends, you will look back at the end of your journey, and you will say, "It is good that I took it as the second guidepost; how exciting, keep going."

And from our perspective, and this is very important, it does not matter how old you are. We see people of all ages reading these transmissions. Regardless of your age, there is a great adventure to be had if you perceive fear the way we ask you to. And in fact, we will leave you with this: If you are not feeling any fear in your life, then perhaps there is a problem. It means you are too comfortable, and maybe you need to expand.

If you are too comfortable, then your expansion is limited. But if you allow yourself to go out of your comfort zone, then all will be well. We are not asking you to jump out of an airplane. ☺ We *are* asking you to do things that make you feel a little uncomfortable in a good way. Blessings, friends.

CHAPTER 39

The Human Experience

Hello, friends. We want to remind you, in every moment you find yourself participating in, you bring your own personal frequency to it. *It* does not bring a frequency to you. You bring your own frequency to *it*.

And so it is; life is life, yes? You might be participating in an experience that is not to your liking. You might even say to yourself, "I am suffering." We want to acknowledge, friends, as the channel has wanted us to do for some time, that yes, there is what you might label as suffering that can be part of the life experience. But no matter what moment you find yourself in, no matter what it is you find yourself observing or participating in, you *can* bring your own personal frequency into it.

Your personal frequency is not found in the suffering, though. No, it is not found there. It is found inside you.

Always retreat into *that*. When you do *that*, you will make a subtle shift in vibration that helps you move toward what you might define as a better outcome. If you plug-in, and you make a very subtle shift in your personal frequency, in your vibration, and you bring *that* to the table, you bring *that* to the moment that is at hand, then things begin to shift.

We, personally, do not like this word that many of you use, suffering. Yet, if that is your preference, then we will accept it. But we tell you to close your eyes, to go within, to bring your own personal frequency to the moment, and you will begin to lift yourself up out of the suffering, no matter what it is. This is the path, friends, that we offer you today. In this way, there is a greater likelihood that tomorrow you will feel more uplifted than you do today. And even if your body does not feel uplifted, you will still feel uplifted because of your commitment to raise your vibration as high as possible in each and every moment of your life experience.

Do you see what we are doing, friends? We are empowering you to have the most easeful and the most pleasurable life experience possible, even while acknowledging there may very well be suffering. And in this way, we are making our teachings complete and whole for the channel so that he feels nothing has been left out. He does not want people asking, "What about this? What about that?" So, we are doing our best to make our teachings as complete and whole as possible and to honor the entire human experience.

CHAPTER 39 - THE HUMAN EXPERIENCE

We will leave you with this because we feel like we have said enough about this. Today, the channel says, "I am feeling miserable. I am not feeling well. My body does not feel as good as I would like it to feel. My mood is not the best." And he is even, on a very subtle level, saying that it is not fair.

But we tell him he has his practice, that he can raise his vibration, and he can bring *that* to the experience he is having. It will become a more easeful experience. It will put him on a new trajectory toward feeling better in his body and having a better mood. This is the practice we offer you, acknowledging you might have your day, or your days when you might say you are suffering, or you are feeling this or that.

And we tell you that all you seek is within you. So, you may go *there*; you may find the support you are seeking there. It comes by connecting to your heart-space and raising. Then, you open your eyes, and even if it is very subtle, there will be a shift. And from our perspective, even a very subtle shift in the right direction is like moving into a new flow, from one river to another. And the river you transition to, by way of a subtle shift in vibration, leads to another river, and then another, and then another. And things improve.

And even if it is time to leave your body, and you are experiencing *that* kind of suffering, it can become an easier experience by taking root in that which is within you. And though we have spoken quite a bit about physical suffering in this transmission, we speak of *all* kinds of suffering. This practice is applicable to every moment your mind might deem as unsatisfactory to you. Do not fight it. Go within yourself. Raise your own vibration. Bring *that* to the moment, and that will create the subtle shift that is needed to move you in the right direction.

And now we will leave you with this. If you feel like you have fallen so far down the well that there is no way out, then it is OK to ask for help. But make sure the person you ask for help does not have their own agenda. Their only agenda should be to liberate you from whatever low-vibrational experience you are having. Their only purpose for helping you should be because they have unconditional divine love for you, and that is it.

We remind you, friends, we are all here to serve each other in this way and to lift each other up. If you do not feel like the help you need is coming, then pray for it. This is where prayer can be helpful.

CHAPTER 40

Sacred Moments

Hello, friends. Do you see that your heart space is always calling you home? If you are not in it, you might find you feel quite lonely. On the one hand, we are making a joke. But on the other hand, it is quite true. You need to be in the company of your heart to feel good, just as it is nice to be in the company of others to feel good.

We encourage you to, first, be in communion with your own heart center, and then, be in communion with others.

For the experience of being with others will be much more pleasurable if you are in your heart. We tell you, friends, that the experience of your day will be completely different if you choose to be in your heart before you begin and in every moment during your day. Every interaction will be more fruitful and more pleasurable. And most importantly, every interaction you have will serve the purpose of creation, which is to share the love you have in your heart with others. It does not take much to share it, friends.

Today, we are speaking of the ordinary interactions that you have with everybody around you that you might pass by without giving any thought to, but that are all sacred. Do you see that every time you come into contact with another human being or any other life form on this planet, that it is a sacred moment? It cannot be any other way. For how can it be that you come into contact with an aspect of the creator and do not consider that moment to be sacred? These moments that you might label as quite *ordinary*, that you might attempt to get through as quickly as possible, are not ordinary moments at all. They are *sacred* moments!

And thus, we invite you to bring sacredness into every moment of every day. And you do that by being in your heart, by listening with your heart, and by expressing with your heart. Some of you listen with your ears, and you express with your mouth. ☺ Yet, we encourage you now, as you step forward along this path we are outlining, to first listen with your heart and to then express yourself through your heart so that everything is moving through your heart. This is how life is meant to be.

Some of you must move *up* through the chakra system, and others of you must move *down* through the chakra system to get there. What we mean is there are *some* who

CHAPTER 40 - SACRED MOMENTS

listen and respond with their minds. That means you are *disconnected* from the pleasure of being in your heart. And there are others who might listen and respond by way of their second chakra, which is their reproductive area, and that has them thinking they are still in the jungle, fighting for survival of the species. ☺ We are laughing. It is meant to be humorous and not taken too seriously.

Do you see that when you come from your heart, that is where the pleasure is, that is where the joy is, that is where the fulfillment is, that is where the connection to your god-self and the connection to others' god-selves is present? So, we have given you the practice of sacred retreat to learn how to still your mind and to experience your heart, to experience the great love that is within you and that you have for all others. That is the purpose of sacred retreat.

The channel was at a meditation class recently. He was very curious about what another teacher offered. And the teacher asked, "What is the definition of meditation?" Well now, we just told you from our perspective. And if the channel himself is teaching a meditation class, he will ask that same question. And he will give his students the answer we have given, which comes from our perspective and his.

Now that you have that practice, bring it into your day with you. Certainly, the practice (sacred retreat) *itself* might become pleasurable. In fact, if we have not said this before, we will say it now. It is likely it will become so pleasurable you will want to sit for very long periods of time because you will feel blissful and even ecstatic as you experience the great love and the great light within you.

And then, so it is, friends, if you see someone meditating, and they tell you they are enlightened, or they are a meditation master, but they do not have a smile on their face, perhaps you can entertain, without judgment, the notion that they might not be! ☺ We are laughing. For ultimately, with practice, the sacred retreat is one that should put a smile on your face. We are asking you to take your practice out into the world with you. And as we have said before, to see through the eyes of god, and to see, listen, and speak through your heart center.

We want to give you some examples of how you can do this. We are going to take some moments from the channel's life yesterday to demonstrate it. He went to get his guitar repaired. He got a smoothie at a coffee shop. He got groceries at the grocery store. You might consider these to be ordinary moments. But from our perspective, they are not moments when your phone, or other things that are going on around you, or the noise in your head should distract you.

Rather, they are *sacred* moments for you to connect with the other person you are interacting with in a heartfelt way. And if you sense their vibration is low, that they are having a bad day, that they are experiencing something in their life that is troubling, you will pick up on that simply by tuning into their energy. Then, your responsibility is to hold a space of love for that person to reside in, to smile, to be extra nice even if that person is not being nice in return. Do you see that when you do *that*, you will uplift the other person? Then, you are serving your purpose.

Many of you have what we call big dreams. Some of them might be related to your soul contract. We are not persuading you to turn away from these. What we *are* encouraging you to do is to realize that *every* moment is a moment when you can serve the purpose of creation. So do not miss the moments. For even if you are the person who says to themselves, "I am having a bad day. I am experiencing something troubling in my life. My vibration is low," or whatever it is, *still*, we encourage you to do as we are encouraging you to do. Because if you choose to see, to listen, and to speak from your heart, you will uplift yourself.

Do you see, friends, that when you follow this guidance we are giving you, you not only serve creation by uplifting others, but you uplift yourself as well? Part of the creator's desire is for you to see and experience every moment as sacred. And we tell you that we, the Teachers of the Light, have full permission to speak on the creator's behalf. For we are an extension of the creator. And yes, we are talking about *that* creator, the one many of you label as god. We are an extension of *that*.

We are *all* extensions of that, friends. It just so happens that from our vantage point, from where we reside vibrationally, we can see things with a little more clarity. We can see things without all the filters that obstruct true vision. And we share things with you from this perspective, from this vibration, from this plane of being, or from whatever it is you would like to label it.

We do not like to say we are closer to the creator than you are, friends, because we are not. You can be as close or as far away as you choose to be. This is important for you to understand. We actually encourage you to read that sentence again:

> *You can be as close or as far away as you want to be.*

Right now, you might not believe it. There might be many filters in place that prevent you from experiencing that truth. But we say it because we know the possibility is present for you to *awaken* to the truth as we see it.

And it is by way of your sacred retreat practice and by every other practice that we share with you that you begin to awaken to the truth that you are not nearly as far away from the creator as you think you are, that you are actually much closer. In fact, for some of you, who stick to the path, you might find one day that you awaken to your own truth that there is no separation at all, that you are not far away, *and* you are not close. You are actually one with the creator.

The channel has days when he experiences himself as close. Perhaps, he even dips his toes into the oneness at times. But we predict that there will come a day for him and for many of you when you will know, experientially through your practice of sacred retreat and every other

CHAPTER 40 - SACRED MOMENTS

practice we share with you, that you are one with and not separate from your source.

So, friends, we have ended this transmission with quite an advanced teaching, one that points to the truth of your being-ness. That is what we label as an advanced teaching. We will end there for this particular transmission. And we encourage you to re-read it. This is a very important practice we shared with you. It fulfills the purpose of creation when you experience every moment as sacred—when you come to realize that every moment *is* sacred and treat it that way. May your day be *filled* with sacredness. Blessings, friends.

CHAPTER 41

Laughter Is the Best Medicine

The next transmission is from a Native American group of guides, the Council of Elders.

Hello! ☺ We are laughing. We enjoy laughing like you do. It is true what they say. Laughter is the best medicine we know. There are many medicines on your planet, many more today than there were in our time. You can go to the drugstore and choose from millions of medications to do this and to do that. But laughter is the best kind. This is why the channel is drawn to things that make him laugh. He knows.

We encourage you to do the same. Find a way to bring more laughter into your life. Even if you are going to gather with some friends for 'silly night' and say, "OK, tonight is the night we are going to be silly together. This is just what we are going to do." The channel needs this, too. He takes life too seriously sometimes. But there are many around him helping him to loosen up and to enjoy life more.

Sometimes you have to *let* yourself laugh. And you know what we mean by that. You wrap yourself up tight because you say to yourself, "I am an adult. Life is serious. I have all these responsibilities and obligations." If you are not laughing, I say, you are not really living. So please make time for laughter in your life.

Many of you, the channel himself included, have so many goals, "I must do this. I must do that." Wow! I am glad I am not in a body right now. ☺ I am joking. Do not worry. You are blessed to be in a body. It is a blessing to be in human form. It is as simple as that. But why don't you make laughter goal number one? It is the most important goal. Some of you have not laughed in a long time. It is time. It is time for laughter. Find somebody you can laugh with.

If you do not have a friend you can laugh with, find one. The channel is thinking of posting on the internet for a friend whom *he* can laugh with. This is not a bad idea, but we say pray for it. If you want a friend to laugh with, pray for it. It will come. It is that simple. But do not pray for it once or twice and then forget about your prayer. Pray for it every day until it shows up on your doorstep—until your laughing friend shows up on your doorstep. Then, you will know prayer works. Why not make it a fun game? Pray for

CHAPTER 41 - LAUGHTER IS THE BEST MEDICINE

someone to laugh with and see if that person shows up in your life. If they do not, then you can return the book. ☺

I am Indian Chief. The channel has asked me for a name. But I kind of like this name Indian Chief because it sounds silly to me. I am the Indian Chief! I bid you farewell now. I will see you again soon. Adios, amigos! Oh, you are getting to know my sense of humor now, perhaps. And maybe you are saying to yourself, well, *you* are somebody I would like to be laughing friends with. Well, if the channel is bold enough to channel for more groups of people, then you can be laughing friends with me and the channel together. We will all laugh at the same time.

This would be very fun!

CHAPTER 42

Falling in Love

Hello, dear ones. If you have read as we have guided you to read, taking your time to fully digest each teaching, taking your time to embody the truth and the guidance inherent in each of them, then it is likely that much time has passed since you began reading this book. If you are here too quickly, meaning if only a week or two has gone by since you first began the book, it might be in your best interest to return to the beginning and to really take your time with it. For there are some of you out there who have done *that*. ☺ We are laughing. You know who you are, yes? The ones who have said to themselves, "Well, this is delightful, but I will just keep going." This book was never meant to be like that, friends.

These teachings are a practice, friends.

Do you see that? They are not something you read and then leave behind you much in the way you would watch a movie or read a novel. Every practice we have shared with you must be embodied on a daily basis. And for that reason, it might be necessary for you to go back many times and reread many times. For each of these teachings has many layers. And it could be that you read the same teaching multiple times, and that each time, you discover something new because you graduated to the next level of awareness, and you can see more clearly the truth embodied in the teaching. It is even like this for the channel. He was editing one of these chapters recently, and he said, "Oh, yes, I forgot all about this practice. This is very relevant to my life right now. I will get back to it."

So, even though this book is coming to a close soon, we encourage you to put it in a place where you can easily see it and refer to it as your divine blueprint for life. This is what it is meant to be. It is meant to guide you in the direction you are meant to go.

Where is that, you might say? It is toward everything you seek that is already within you. It is the peace that you seek. It is the harmony that you seek. It is the *joy* you seek. It is the *bliss* you seek. It is the love you seek.

Too often, many of you look for this love outside yourselves as the channel has done.

CHAPTER 42 - FALLING IN LOVE

We tell you, until you discover the great love within you, it cannot appear in front of you. And if it does, well, it might not last very long. It might not be very harmonious for a long period of time. It might fall apart quickly. But the lasting love you seek in your lives will appear once you discover the love within you.

And perhaps the *form* the love takes will not last forever because *that* is impossible. But the love *itself*? That can last forever. That never has to end at all. Once you are in love, there is no need to ever leave it. That is a very important statement, friends. We'll say it again: Once you are in love, there is no need to ever leave it.

You needn't fall *in* love and then *out* of love. You can always be *in* love. This is the state of being we are guiding you back toward, a state of love that is not dependent on whether there is a form outside you to give your love to. This is the illusion that much of humanity is struggling with. We will say it directly: There is nothing you need that is outside yourself. And yet, the irony is that if you *are* seeking something, if you *are* seeking love that is outside yourself, once you truly grasp through direct experience that it is not needed because what you are seeking is *within* you, then it will mysteriously appear outside you as well.

And you might say then that you will be doubly fulfilled. ☺ You will be fulfilled by the love within yourself. And you will be fulfilled by taking delight in the pleasure of love outside yourself as an added bonus.

How many times have you said to yourself, "Oh, I need

this that exists outside myself." And then you get it. And then down the road, you say to yourself, "Oh, I didn't really need it. What I needed was what will always be inside me." This is the teaching here, friends. This is what we are getting at.

This is one of those high-level teachings that you will need to read many times. Perhaps through a course of time that might last months or even years. Because the more you connect and find yourself absorbed in what's within you, the more it will make sense because you will have the direct experience to back it up. You will have the direct experience to know the words we speak through the channel are true.

Perhaps you do not have that direct experience *yet*. But you will. By way of your sacred retreat, by way of your spiritual practice, you shall have that experience. And you will know what we already know and what the channel is *beginning* to discover. ☺ You notice how we highlight that word *beginning*. That's because he is not fully absorbed in the completeness and wholeness of the god-presence within him. And he is still doing a little seeking outside himself. But we tell him, no, sit, go within. What you need is within you. This is the path you must follow, friends. In, then, out. Discover what you wish to discover outside yourself, inside yourself first.

CHAPTER 43

Now Is the Time

Hello, friends. As always, we meet you in the space of the heart, for that is the only space where we can truly meet. That is the only space within which *we* can experience ourselves. And it is the only space within which *you* can truly experience yourself. And so it is, friends, if you are to ever pick up this book and find you are not quite settled in to *that* space, then put it down, close your eyes, and settle into this space. *Then*, open your eyes and read the words we speak.

There has been a long period of silence for the channel between the last sentence and this one. And it is because he, *too*, is still learning how to settle into his heart as a precedent for receiving the words we speak through him. And this is what we ask of you, as well. The channel is even remembering why we are in his life, to bring him back into his heart space that at times seems a little bit elusive to him. Or should we say that it is challenging for him to stay there, in his heart space, for long periods of time without interruption. And yet today, this morning, he is beginning to settle back in. So, this is good.

> *It is by way of the heart that you find all you are seeking.*

Dear ones, we tell you, no matter what is going on in your lives, no matter how far away from your heart you are, no matter how many thoughts are in the way, there is always a path that is available to you to come back home. For the channel, it is very often as simple as sitting, closing his eyes, noticing his breath, and allowing his heart to shine so brightly that the thoughts dissolve.

We have encouraged you and continue to encourage you to do this practice. But we also encourage you to do *any* practice that brings you back home. Perhaps, it is sitting with a pet. Perhaps, it is reminding yourself of what you're grateful for. Perhaps, it is simply going outside and allowing the sun's brightness to shine on your face. Whatever it is, do *that*. And then, carry on with your day.

We are going to say something bold. Perhaps, we have said it before in another way, or even with similar words, "If you are present in your heart center, then you *are* where you are meant to be no matter where you are physically." We repeat:

CHAPTER 43 - NOW IS THE TIME

If you are present in your heart center, then you are where you are meant to be no matter where you are physically.

And it is by way of being present and being in your heart center that your path will unfold in the highest and best way. It is by being present and in your heart center that your spirit, that the universe, that your angels, that your guides, that the creator, will guide you to the experiences you are meant to have.

So *always*, friends, start there. Start inside before going out. Even if you are going to make a list of your goals and the disciplined action steps you need to take to accomplish them, do *that* from a state of presence, settled into your heart center, free from the filters of your mind that often obscure it.

And even if you *think* you know what the next step is, for example, I must do this, or I must do that, be very receptive to what your *spirit* wants to tell you rather than what your mind wants to tell you. Your mind will tell you what it thinks. Your spirit will tell you what is true. We repeat:

Your mind will tell you what it thinks. Your spirit will tell you what is true.

The channel likes this so much he is already planning to put it up on social media today. ☺ The channel is learning how to do this now. Before he steps into the world to act, he sits in a state of receptivity that can only come about through the practice of sacred retreat, the practice of stilling the mind, the practice of tuning in to the heart. Then, he receives the guidance. It comes from within him. It is like a little intuitive nudge. For him, it comes via clairaudience. For you, it might come in a different way. But it comes. And even though the voice might be quiet, it is there to guide him. And because the voice *is* quiet, it requires this receptivity that can only be found through the spiritual practices we've shared.

And then it is that the mind might have been planning or thinking to do this or that. But the spirit, *your* spirit, will guide you in a different direction. Your spirit will tell you what you are truly meant to be doing in the moment. And then, friends, your life can unfold in a way that is better than expected because you are making yourself more available to more synchronicity in your life. And at first, it might *appear* to you that the synchronicities are quite small and irrelevant. But each synchronicity leads to another.

And if you trace your steps back to what we said earlier in this teaching, and you are present, and in your heart, for each step you take along the journey, without any judgment as to where you are in the particular moment, then you are creating the space for your path to unfold in a way that will be quite pleasing to you.

We will leave you with this, friends. The channel has been learning there are certain patterns of behavior that

CHAPTER 43 - NOW IS THE TIME

are not his, that are not his soul's. They come from a belief system that is etched deep within him through experiences he had when he was significantly younger. We will simply label this belief system by saying that it says, "I cannot." But he can, and you can, as well.

Whatever it is you feel inspired to do, whatever it is your soul is calling you to do during this great time of awakening, to serve yourself in a pleasing way, and to serve humanity at the same time, you can do it. You can, and you will. If you believe that you can't, then you're likely to sabotage yourself—because of the fear—because of the doubt.

Ask yourselves what your spirit is capable of. And just for today, can you say I can and I will? Can you say I will take the step, the disciplined action step that is necessary to accomplish what I know I can accomplish? To accomplish what I came here to do? To fulfill my soul's purpose and my soul's mission? Because we know you can, friends. We see it.

So, when you sit in your sacred retreat and you feel a pull from your spirit to move in a particular direction, to do something exciting, to do something that fulfills your purpose, do not discard it a day or two later because of a belief system that tells you that you cannot do it or that you are not worthy of receiving it. Do not do *that*.

Know that all the greatness you need is within you to fulfill the purpose you are here to fulfill. If you were not capable, then you would not be here. It's that simple. Trust yourselves, friends. Trust the inspiration that comes from within. And if you sit long enough and become receptive, you will receive it.

And then, do not doubt it. Do not doubt yourself. And if you *are* doubting yourself, carry on anyway until you doubt yourself no longer. For when you step back, and you see the creation you have manifested by believing in yourself, then you will doubt no more. Trust in things unseen. Trust that the work you are doing in the present moment will lead to the fulfillment of what it is you wish to see and experience.

It is as if you are the director of a film, and you are directing the present moment. Perhaps you do not know how the film will look when it is complete. Perhaps you even have doubts about whether you can complete it and create the masterpiece you wish to create. But you shoot the shot anyway because you have faith, because you have trust, and because you believe in yourself. And then, one day, the masterpiece is complete. And you get to watch the film.

This is the experience you seek to have. You get to watch the film, and you're the star. It is quite magnificent because you believed in yourself enough to do it, to fully participate in each scene of the film, even *if* there was a little doubt, and even *if* the belief in yourself was a little shaky.

It is quite magnificent because you believed strongly enough in your purpose for being here on the planet, and you believed in the inspiration that was bubbling up inside of you. You believed in it enough to follow it. And you

CHAPTER 43 - NOW IS THE TIME

believed in it enough to question the self-doubt and to question the belief systems that were not serving you. And you didn't believe in them to the extent they prevented you from moving forward along your path and from fulfilling your destiny.

Now is the time, friends. Do not delay. When will there be a better time than today? Now is the time to listen to the calling of your heart, to fulfill your purpose on this planet, and to say yes to it, to say yes, unequivocally. Now is the time to believe in yourself so much that any doubts you have take a backseat because you are fully connected to your purpose, to your greatness, to *knowing* what you can create as part of your life experience. And may you create something that is not only pleasing to yourself but that also touches the hearts and souls of humanity in a very purposeful, meaningful way. Blessings, friends.

CHAPTER 44

Conscious Creation

Hello, friends. The channel enjoys acting quite a bit. Yet, at the same time, he feels overwhelmed with everything else he is doing in his life. And he was questioning, and he said, "Is it valuable? Is it worth it to follow this path I enjoy?" And we said yes, it is worth it, but not if it is only self-serving. It must please yourself and tickle yourself. But most importantly, it must touch the hearts and souls of humanity in a purposeful, meaningful way. Otherwise, the work that you are doing is selfish.

If you are a chef—if you are a pastry chef, and you are making desserts only for yourself, what is the point? ☺ But if you are making desserts for everyone, well, that is purposeful. So, we speak to *all those* who are creating what we call works of art. We speak to all the artists out there. Many of you who are reading this book are artistic, even if you do not know you are yet. You are all artists in a way.

We say let the art you create and that you participate in be art that transforms the planet in a positive way. Let it be more than just entertainment. Let it be more than something that pleases you. Let it be art that truly impacts the hearts and souls of people in a beneficial way.

This is the true purpose of art friends. It is not solely there for entertainment. It must hit the heart. It should make you laugh. It should give you a greater understanding of what love is. And if it is going to make you cry, let it be because it is opening your heart in a new and beautiful way. If you are going to read something, if you are going to watch something, let it be *this* type of material, not the other kind. And you know which kind we are talking about. And if you are going to *make* art, let it be the positive kind. And let it be a participatory experience. This is where the joy of being an artist comes from. Create with like-minded, heart-centered individuals who share your vision, who share your purpose.

When you gather together with others in this way, your art can be received by more people. If you choose to go at it alone, it might be a bit of a struggle. It might not be that enjoyable. But if you invite others to participate with you in your vision of creating art that transforms the world, then you will gather energy together. You will gather momentum. You will gather speed. And the universe will support you in ways that you cannot fathom right now.

For those of you who say this is not relevant to me, who

CHAPTER 44 - CONSCIOUS CREATION

say I am not an artist, we say you are. If you are present on this planet, you are a creator. It is as simple as that. The power is within you to create, and you are creating with every step you take. You are creating something. So, in every moment of your life, create something beautiful. Create something that touches the hearts and souls of others.

If you choose to wear a T-shirt that inspires another human being, then you are an artist, are you not? If you choose to smile at another human being in a heartfelt way, then you are an artist, are you not? If you are a homemaker, and you choose to place certain objects in your home in a certain way that touch the hearts and souls of others in a positive way, then you are an artist, are you not?

Do you see what we mean, friends? Even if you do not label yourself as an artist the way many do, you are still an artist. Create from your heart. And do not be shy about sharing what you have created with the world. There is great power in the sharing. There is great fulfillment that occurs when you share something purposeful and meaningful with the world. Many blessings, friends.

CHAPTER 45

Be Receptive

Hello, friends. You are more than just our friends. You are our loved ones. For we love you all dearly. And our love extends to every one of you. No matter where you are, no matter what you are doing, our love is present with you as we speak through the channel. This is how it goes. There is nowhere that our love is not. But you must become receptive to it if you would like to experience it.

> *Receptivity cannot happen in the doing. It cannot.*

You must sit back. You must relax. And you must allow yourself to receive what the universe wants to give to you. It could be a very simple moment of noticing a bird, or noticing a tree, or noticing that you are receiving the breath of life. But it must be received in a state of reception.

And so, we ask you, friends, if you are seeking love, why is it then that you focus on a lack of it? For if you are doing that, then you are closing yourself off to receiving it. Do you see what we mean when we say that?

We are going to give you a very specific example from the channel's life. This afternoon he went to a coffee shop. And he noticed a beautiful woman with a child. And he thought to himself despondingly, "Hmm... I wonder if she is single because she is quite attractive." He was focusing on the lack of love in his life, the lack of a partner. And we tell him that this is not the way to *receive* the love he wants. We say it to you, too. The way to *receive* is to be in a state of reception and to focus on what it is you are *receiving* from the universe, not what you are lacking. You are lacking nothing at all. We want to repeat that because it is very important: You are lacking nothing at all. All of god is already present within you. So, how could you lack anything at all? It is only because of your separation from the source within you that you *think* you are lacking, but you are not.

This is a rather advanced teaching, friends. But you get it, do you not? For you have made great strides through your life experience and your spiritual practice that has elevated your consciousness to a state that allows you to be receptive to this teaching and to understand it. And now it is the time to embody it, to focus on the goodness that is around you that is being received by you in every moment of your life experience. Thus, you lift yourself up from what you call your suffering, and you begin to receive the bounty of the universe.

And so it is, we are asking the channel, and we are asking *you*, to have yet another day of reception. Choose a day and let it be your intention to be in a state of reception, to be receiving all the gifts around you. Do not look for it. Simply be present to it. Start with your breath. And if you can get nowhere else but that, that is suitable. Be aware you are receiving your breath. Take pleasure in that. And then you can say, "Oh wow, yes, I am receiving my breath. What else am I receiving?" This is how you create a shift in your life—from looking around you and thinking that you do not have what it is you need, what it is you want, to actually being in the flow of *receiving* what it is you want.

It does not take much to make the shift. It is a shift in vibration. It is a shift in consciousness. And it all leads to the fulfillment of what it is you are seeking that is already within you. Do you see that if you want to receive love, for example (and this applies to everything you want), that you hinder yourself by looking around you and saying, "I do not have it. I want it." It's much more fruitful for you to say, "Look at all I am receiving in this present moment. I am receiving my breath. I am receiving the food that has been gifted to me by the beautiful planet I am living on."

Do you see where we are going with this, friends? Continue in *this* direction, and then you will see. You will begin to magically receive more of what it is you seek because you are in a state of reception.

The channel, even though he has been on the path for quite some time, has a part of his mind that does not believe it. He does not believe what it is we are telling him. So, we say OK, be the scientist if that is what is needed. Try it out for a day or two. It might not be that the life of your dreams appears in front of you. It might not be that you suddenly win the lottery! ☺ It might not be that all your dreams come true. But we tell you, if you begin to receive, rather than focusing on what it is you are not receiving, which is a trick of the mind, then little by little, you will *indeed* begin to receive. And that will give you more confidence to know you are on the right road and to keep going with it.

For some of you, it is impossible to apply this teaching to your life because you are in a constant state of doing. And if you are constantly focused on the doing, then you are not receiving. This is why your spiritual practice is so incredibly important. It is actually the training ground that begins to teach you how to sit, how to relax, and how to be receptive. Give that gift to yourself, friends.

If you are one of those who cannot receive this teaching because you are in the constant state of doing, let the doing go. Find little moments here and there to let it go. And begin to receive. May you receive all that you wish to receive. Yes, may you receive all that is in your vortex and waiting for you to receive, as another channel puts it. Make the shift to receiving. Let god give you what god wants to give you.

CHAPTER 45 - BE RECEPTIVE

What the channel is experiencing is that for a moment, he will believe *that*. He will allow himself to become receptive, to receive. And yet, a day or two later, he will not believe it anymore. He will grow tired of the waiting. He will say, "Where is it? I do not have it yet." ☺ Be wary of this trick of the mind, friends. Stay in a state of reception. Notice if your mind is beginning to trick you by doubting it. And then settle back into your state of reception. Then, the gifts will begin to *flow*. And their flow will increase.

We will leave you with this, friends. If you see something you would like, instead of focusing on the lack of it, say, "Thank you! I know this is coming into *my* life soon. Thank you." It will create a noticeable *shift* in the way you are feeling. It will make your day more pleasurable. And you will continue to stay in the state of reception you are meant to stay in. That is it for today. Blessings.

CHAPTER 46

A Momentous Occasion

Blessings, dear ones. Many times in this book, we have spoken of going within and its importance. Once you have done that, it is time to take what you have learned in your sacred retreat, and to share it with others. And this is what we are asking the channel to do. And, of course, we ask you to do the same. Whatever it is you have gained from your practice of sacred retreat, from going within time and time again, it is not meant just for you. At first, it might be. But then you must share it with others. You are selfish if you keep it to yourself, especially during this awakening when so many need your light. So, we encourage you to be *brave* and to share it.

Many of you are saying, "Yes, you are speaking to me. I have much to share, and I am a little afraid to share it." And we say we honor your humanity and the doubt that comes along with it. But regardless, now is the time to begin to share what is within you and what is meant to be shared. Now is the time to contribute *fully* to the great awakening that is occurring on the planet so that when the time comes for your spirit to leave your body, you can say with the last words you speak that when doubt was present, you stepped forward anyway, showed up to the party, and did what was necessary to serve your purpose. This is what we are asking of the channel. And this is what we are asking of *all* of you.

> *Now is the time. There is no better time to begin to share what is within you.*

And then yes, you go back within. This is the process. Do you see it now? You go in, and you go out. And each time you go out, you go out with a bit more to share by way of your own personal experience, by way of what you have experienced in your sacred retreat. And it is a process, friends. It will never be up to the expectations of your ego right away. It will not. Afterward, your ego might say, "Well, I could've done better." Yes, of course, you could have because you are learning. This is what you are here to do. You are here to learn through your experience. Do not be afraid to learn as you go along.

Here is an analogy, a silly one. Hopefully, it will make you laugh. If you are in the second grade, well then, we say you have much to share with those who are beneath you in the first grade. And if you are in the third grade, then you

CHAPTER 46 - A MOMENTOUS OCCASION

have much to share with those who are beneath you in the second grade. Do you see? And while you are sharing in the third grade, you might think to yourself, "Oh wow, I am only in the third grade. When I am in a different grade, it will be much better." This is what the ego does. But you are more than equipped to share right now, wherever it is you are on your journey. Hopefully, you see what we are saying with this analogy.

Wherever it is you are on the journey, it is time to share so you can lift others up who are beneath you. By this, we simply mean they have not *awakened* to what is within them quite yet, to the degree you have. You are all equal in our eyes. The light of god shines equally within you all. This is the core of our teaching. Let's repeat it: The light of the creator shines equally within all. It does not matter what you look like. It does not matter what your religion is. It does not even matter what your beliefs are. The light of the creator shines equally within all beings everywhere. And we truly mean all beings—without exclusion, without discrimination, and without segregation.

That is all that we have for today, friends. There are a few more teachings that have yet to come through the channel. However, we are going to make a bold statement and say this will be the final chapter in the book. Additional transmissions will be placed in the book in their appropriate spots. This particular chapter is here to serve as a final reminder of all the guidance we have offered you. And we feel quite content in saying that it is all present.

And so now, friends, we bid you farewell. We will be back. We are laughing as the channel is reminded of a Terminator movie when the lead character says, "I'll be back." ☺ As the channel continues to raise his vibration, different energies will begin to come through. And these new energies will have more to offer. If you were to look at this as school, and you were to perceive us as your teachers, we are very high vibrationally. Yet, there will be even more advanced teachings that begin to come through the channel as he progresses along his path. We will all progress together. That is what we are here to do.

We look forward to being with you again in the next book and through other ways that we will introduce to you. And what we are speaking of in particular are the other opportunities you will have to interact with us, online or in person. And this is where the channel becomes a little reluctant, where his ego chimes in, "I am not ready for that. I would prefer to stay alone. Let it just be the three of us—me, the energies that are coming through me, and the phone that is doing the recording. Let it be the three of us." ☺

But we are saying he is ready, and you are too, to take the next step forward in the journey. Celebrate and rejoice, friends. It is a great time to be alive during this shift of consciousness that is occurring for all humanity as we speak these words. When you read them, when this material is published, the consciousness of the planet will have shifted again. For it will continue to shift until all know themselves

CHAPTER 46 - A MOMENTOUS OCCASION

for who they are. Until all know the great love and the great light that is within them, and until the creator's vision of heaven becoming manifest on planet Earth becomes *fully* manifest for all to experience. Blessings, friends.

Note from Author: The guides asked me to include one final chapter in the book. It can be found here as a bonus chapter:

https://www.awakenwithdarren.com/bonus-chapter

About the Author

Darren Marc is an internationally recognized healer and teacher with over fifteen years of experience in the field of self-growth and mind/body/soul wellness. As a yoga teacher and Reiki practitioner, he's impacted the lives of thousands, helping his clients achieve happier and more spiritually fulfilled lives through his workshops and lessons.

As the author of *Journey of the Heart*, a powerful guide on the topic of spiritual wellness and self-discovery, Darren is dedicated to sharing the wisdom of his guides and improving the lives of the people around him. He's also worked as a former writer at *For Your Health Magazine*.

In his free time, Darren enjoys singing and composing songs, working as a realtor, and being an ambassador for the non-profit group *Yoga Gives Back*.

For more information about Darren and his workshops, visit **awakenwithdarren.com**.

For new video transmissions from The Teachers of The Light, join the private Facebook group **www.facebook.com/groups/journeyoftheheartbook**

EMAIL: DarrenMarc111@gmail.com

WEBSITE: www.awakenwithdarren.com

PRIVATE FACEBOOK GROUP:
www.facebook.com/groups/journeyoftheheartbook

www.ingramcontent.com/pod-product-compliance
Lightning Source LLC
Chambersburg PA
CBHW071957290426
44109CB00018B/2053